The Trust
Paradigm

The Trust
Paradigm

Geoff Hudson-Searle
Mark Herbert

Matador
Unit E2 Airfield Business Park,
Harrison Road, Market Harborough,
Leicestershire. LE16 7UL
Tel: 0116 2792299
Email: books@troubador.co.uk
Web: www.troubador.co.uk/matador
Twitter: @matadorbooks

ISBN 978 1803133 188 (Hardback)
ISBN 978 1803133 195 (Paperback)

British Library Cataloguing in Publication Data.
A catalogue record for this book is available from the British Library.

Printed and bound in the UK by TJ Books Limited, Padstow, Cornwall
Typeset in 11pt Aldine401 BT by Troubador Publishing Ltd, Leicester, UK

Matador is an imprint of Troubador Publishing Ltd

We would like to thank Jackie Rice, Marcela Murillo and our good friend Sophie Sayer for their trust, love and partnership, and our editorial and publishing team in the compilation of the book.

We would also like to acknowledge those who 'came before': Stephen MR Covey, Patrick Lencioni and Simon Sinek.

A special mention to The Honor Foundation, a not-for-profit, providing guidance to members of the US elite military units as they transition to civilian life. For these special operators, trust is truly the currency they trade in and the language they speak. It has been a pure privilege to serve as a career transition coach to a few of these amazing patriots.

We are proud to support Love146 and share their values of trust and hope. We are delighted to be working with Love146 and contributions from the book sales will go to the Love146 charity. This is something close to our hearts. By helping build a trusted family for children, and following them through their journey for as long as they want them to. Love146 embodies that.

Finally, we would like to thank my late grandmother Annette and grandfather George who allowed me to dream and never stop believing in this book. Without their love, support and constant belief, The Trust Paradigm would not have been possible.

CONTENTS

Contents

About the authors

Geoffrey Hudson-Searle

Geoffrey Hudson Searle – Geoff is a serial business advisor , C-suite executive, and digital non-executive director to growth phase companies, and CEO of International Business and Executive Management (IBEM).

Geoff has over 30 years' experience in the business and management arena. He has written five books: *Freedom After the Sharks*; *Meaningful Conversations*; *Journeys to Success: Volume 9, GOD in Business*; and *Purposeful Discussions.* He lectures at business forums, conferences and is a regular judge at the Lloyds Bank Business Excellence awards. His work has been the focus of TEDx and RT Europe business documentaries across various thought-leadership topics.

Having worked for corporate companies Citibank N.A, MICE Group Plc, Enigma Design, MMT Inc, Kaspersky Laboratory, Bartercard Plc, and RG Group around the world, Geoff has vast international experience working with SME and multinational international clients.

He is a member and fellow of the Institute of Directors, associate of The Business Institute of Management, a co-founder and board member of the Neustar International Security Council

(NISC) and a member of the Advisory Council for The Global Cyber Academy.

International clients with which Geoff has worked include the British Government, HP, Compaq, BT, Powergen, Intel, ARM, Wartsila Group, Atari, Barclays Bank, Societe Generale, Western Union, Chase and Volvo. Geoff has worked in a broad range of industries

Mark F. Herbert

Mark is the practice leader in organizational change and employment brand implementation for the consulting firms New Paradigms LLC and Mark F. Herbert & Associates, Inc.

His educational background includes a BS in Management from Arizona State University and graduate study at the University of Oregon's Institute for Industrial Relations. He is a certified facilitator in both the Achieve Global and Integrity Systems suite of programmes.

Mark has successfully led organizational change initiatives in high technology, health care, financial services and other sectors including an integrated employment branding and organizational branding campaign which resulted in a 50% increase in revenue and recognition for the organization as a top employer for three consecutive years during his tenure there.

He has more than 40 years' experience of managerial, executive, and consulting roles in both for-profit and not-for-profit organizations, from small businesses to Fortune 100 companies; these include Honeywell, Inc, Spectra Physics Scanning, Oregon Community Credit Union, Burley Design,

Forrest Technical Coatings, and Alvord-Taylor, Inc. He has worked in many sectors including high technology, financial services, custom publishing, ecotourism, and health care.

He is a member of the Key Change Institute and adjunct faculty at the Eastern Caribbean Center for Management Development.

Mark is considered an international thought leader in Organizational Development, Employee Engagement, Employment Branding, and Performance Management.

His first book, *Managing Whole People*, has been referred to as 'America's best workforce stimulus plan' and he has an international following for his blog at www.newparadigmsllc.com and his posts on LinkedIn and Bestthinking.com.

Mark lives in Eugene, OR, and is an avid Oregon Ducks and Tennessee Titans fan.

PREFACE

*"Trust is the glue of life. It's the most essential ingredient
in effective communication. It's the foundational principle
that holds all relationships."*

American educator and author, Steven R. Covey.

Covid-19 is a crucible within which resilient leadership
has been refined since the onset of the pandemic in early
2020. Acting without perfect information and no playbook, and
often with only a few hours or days to spare, CEOs have had
to guide their organizations through the myriad of decisions
and challenges that have had significant implications for their
company's whole system: employees, customers, clients,
financial partners, suppliers, investors, and other stakeholders, as
well as for society as a whole.

At the same time, almost everywhere we turn, trust is on
the decline. Trust in our culture at large, in our institutions and
in our companies is significantly lower than a generation ago.
Research commissioned in 2020 by International Business and
Executive Management found that 69 per cent of employees
trust their CEO a little or not at all. Consider the loss of trust and

confidence in the financial markets today. Indeed, trust makes the world go round – and right now we're experiencing a crisis of trust.

In the words of Tom Peters – American writer on business practices – "TRUST, not technology, is the issue of the decade."

In any normality trust is paramount, but given current world events, never has there been more need for increased trust. This simple formula emphasizes the key elements of trust for individuals and for organizations:

$$Trust = Transparency + Relationship + Experience$$

The Trust Paradigm draws on the hard-won truths of two authors, Geoff Hudson-Searle and Mark Herbert, and draws on their deep personal lessons from life and business practice, and their efforts to distil those lessons into principles that lead towards a more purposeful life.

The book is intended to be both a holistic overview of what generates and builds trust, and a hands-on guide to how that can be done. A wide range of tips, models and techniques that will help to build strong and effective trust solutions in today's business world are combined with a range of insights into the topical subjects of the day.

The term 'trust' has been overused forever and, during the last decade, considerably devalued. In this book, the authors aim to take the concept back to its essentials and to re-evaluate how real, meaningful trust can be incorporated into management and leadership.

Although all the chapters in the book are strongly interrelated, for ease of reference it is divided into three key sections: Communications; strategy; and business development and growth. You can start with your particular area of interest, or you can read the book from the first page to the end; there really is a topic for everyone.

The business professionals and individuals dealing with the great challenges of today's disruptive and disrupted business world now have renewed responsibility for what business does best: they must innovate, invest and grow their organizations. Change and transformation can be radical and painful, yet many wait until circumstances force their hand even when they know that change must, and should, come. Whether change has been forced upon you, or whether you are openly seeking and embracing transformation, this book will arm you with tips, advice and techniques to spark fresh thinking about the status quo and inspire the innovation your circumstances demand for the creation of a better business environment.

The Trust Paradigm's lessons are also relevant far beyond the business world. They can support clearer understanding of institutional behaviour for all kinds of people: students, budding entrepreneurs, volunteers, social enterprise organizers – quite simply, anyone who aspires to do better.

INTRODUCTIONS FROM THE AUTHORS

Geoff Hudson-Searle

> *"If I make deposits into an Emotional Bank Account with you through courtesy, kindness, honesty, and keeping my commitments to you, I build up a reserve. Your trust towards me becomes higher, and I can call upon that trust many times if I need to. I can even make mistakes and that trust level, that emotional reserve, will compensate for it. My communication may not be clear, but you'll get my meaning anyway. You won't make me 'an offender for a word'. When the trust account is high, communication is easy, instant, and effective."*
>
> Stephen R. Covey

Promoting the art of listening is what promotes trust.

Towards the end of a recent video call with a client, I noticed a visible physical shift in their body language; they exhaled, dropped their shoulders, and paused. I knew something important was arising within them. I continued to maintain eye contact, I remained still, I stayed with them. There could have been tens of thoughts and feelings happening at this moment in their head and their heart.

Be patient. This is a hallowed space.

I was following the advice of Colin D. Smith, also known as The Listener. He's an executive coach and confidant, facilitator and speaker who is passionate about transforming the way we listen. His calm, attentive and patient way of being enables you to feel seen, heard and understood. It awakens your thinking and inspires you to empathically listen to yourself and others. When he discusses why the road to trust starts with the listening step, he is compelling.

My client looked away, looked back, looked away again and then their gaze returned to my eyes. Then they spoke. Or rather, their words were being spoken from somewhere deep inside. These words were demanding to be shared.

They explained how they had had a troubled childhood, were no longer in a relationship and had not been for some time, and that they were finding life very challenging. I had known of this person before this call but I had not spoken to them before. All this information was shared within the one hour on the call.

"Why would you open up to someone you barely knew, sharing things about your past and current situation?"

Why would this be okay? Trust.

"It feels safe here for me to open up to you."

We have all had that experience. A feeling that, 'I need to say something, to tell someone, to share. It must come out. It is on my mind a lot. I need to talk. I need to be heard.'

Research shows that we are constantly checking/assessing a situation or a person to establish whether it or they are a threat to our safety. We do it all the time and it happens so fast and so many times that we are usually unaware of it. Only if we could press pause and step outside ourselves would we be able to tune in and notice it.

If we could do this, we would also notice that we are endlessly deciding and determining what, if anything, we might say, rehearsing how we might present it, and assessing how much we would be willing to share. Even as we are speaking, we are evaluating the reaction and/or response from the person listening.

For example, I may start to express my sadness at the loss of a family member or the breakdown of my relationship; I may get a little emotional, maybe tearful. How the other person behaves will determine how much more I will choose to reveal.

Not much more, probably, to the person who changes the subject at this point, who makes a joke, or who says 'me too' and then makes the conversation all about them. Or the person who starts to look uncomfortable, loses eye contact, shuffles in their chair, looking for an 'exit'. I may decide in these situations to say nothing more.

But in those rare and memorable moments when we notice that the listener is still with us, their eyes deeply connecting with ours, and who is calm, still, quiet and clearly interested in what we might say next, we are then in a space that looks and feels different from most of our conversations. I may find myself thinking, 'There is something about this person, I can't quite put my finger on it. But if I was to think about it, I would say it was trust.'

All stories which have a happy ending must begin somewhere. In the case of my recent video call, it started even before the call began; it started with the listener.

Imagine: the listener knows the call is about to start soon.

He has no idea what may arise during the conversation as he has no agenda. All he sets out to do, or rather to be, is to be still and quiet enough to be able to see and hear the speaker. He knows that anything he has been working on can be put to one side and can be picked up again when then the call finishes. This hour is for the speaker. He focuses on his breath, noticing the inhale and the exhale, and how it is slowing down. This brings him to the present moment. He smiles.

When the call starts, the interaction between listener and speaker could take a multitude of paths, so the listener opts to go along with the speaker's choice of direction and the conversation begins. His 'antennae' registers the cues from what the speaker says, their body language or, rather, their facial expressions (we are on video, after all) and from the tone and cadence of their speech. For example, some speakers arrive in a blur, speaking loudly and fast, and can take many minutes to fully arrive. Meanwhile, the listener is also checking in with their own inner knowing, their intuition if you will: observing their emotional responses to what they hear and see, and monitoring any other feedback from their senses.

He recognizes that all of these are simply thoughts and notices the way they arise, make themselves known and then fall away again. He continues to return to the present and to remain connected to the speaker, using their steady breathing as an anchor.

He becomes aware that the connection between them is deepening, there is flow in what the speaker is saying and sharing. The initial rush to speak is gone and now there is calm, a thoughtful, measured, considered state.

Why the initial rush to speak? The speaker is conscious of

needing to get all their words out before they are interrupted, possibly because they are not used to being heard. They feel they need to keep thinking, keep speaking; they can sense that the other person wants to speak, is waiting to speak. They need to take a breath, but if they pause, the listener will break in. This is important to them; they need to be heard. Please don't interrupt me.

And I don't. I continue looking, seeing them, hearing them.

When they do finally pause, as they always do, I remain with them. Quietly present. In that silence, in that stillness, it all changes. They know too, they feel it, it runs through their whole body, their whole being.

This is a rare moment. All that fighting for 'airtime' drops away, their tension, their 'fight or flight' impulse recedes. Their thinking returns and kicks in; they feel enlivened, inspired. Their thought processes – at lightning speed, and mostly unconsciously – turn a corner.

Who is this person listening to me, what have they done? I am feeling the connection. I don't even know this person, yet at another level I do. I trust them, and yet I don't trust many people so easily and so quickly. However, all their mannerisms are congruent, and my being is not feeling 'disrupted'; this is trust – yes, I trust them.

Maybe I can go deeper with my thinking, with my sharing, with my opening up to them. Could I? Let me try, let me say some more. They are continuing to look interested. Who does that? They are encouraging me to speak more, they ARE interested. In me, little old me.

Oh, my goodness, I am feeling like I matter, that I belong. Being me is okay. A smile breaks out across my face.

The listener notices all of this. He too, smiles.

What happens now is important. Vital, some might say.

The speaker has dropped their metaphorical armour and they are vulnerable, exposed, open to being hurt.

And where this goes now is all about the intention of the listener.

The intention? Yes.

Because for some, listening is seen as a way to get something, a way to con another. As with anything, there can be a good and a bad side to effective listening, a light and a dark, one that serves or one that takes away. Intention is all, and this is what will either build and retain the trust that's been generated or will destroy that trust and, with it, the relationship.

That is why your intention must be good, every step of the journey. We all have an inbuilt hogwash monitor and, while it is not one hundred per cent accurate all the time, on the whole we instinctively know when something is not right, often picking it up within those first ten seconds of a meeting.

If your intention is good, the trust you generate will rise and deepen as will the relationship. Knowing someone with whom you are confident you can be yourself and share whatever is on your mind is, sadly, uncommon. It is both rare and special to know someone who will listen, not judge, not interrupt, not fix and not offer advice, but will allow you the time and space to think and come to your own conclusions.

Listening is the bedrock on which trust is built. Add in good intention and you have the basis for a deep and ever-deepening relationship.

Trust starts with transparency: telling what you know and admitting what you don't. Trust is also a function of relationships; some level of 'knowing' each other among you and your employees, your customers, and your ecosystem. And knowing, from experience, whether you reliably do what you say.

When we look at the constant and repetitive process of our own thinking, we see how habitually it creates a sense of self and other. The power of storytelling can access unconditioned and untarnishable space of mind; how storytelling can render the mind more pliable and alive with possibility; and the power of fairy tales to move us personally.

Reflecting on this now, I see how it is a perfect example of how stories call to stories. While listening to a story, a child experiences all the emotions that are present: whether it is fear, determination, courage, kindness, or gratitude. Usually, storytelling is the domain of the adult; the teacher, librarian, or parent. Making space for children to tell their own stories acknowledges the value of their experience, while also reinforcing their sense of themselves as able to care for others.

Mindfulness sets the stage for this kind of reciprocal sharing, in which the positive values of friendship are powerfully reinforced, first through the images of the folktale, and then through the children's association of their own life experience with the events of the story they've just heard.

We maintain our world with our inner dialogue. A woman or man of knowledge is aware that the world will change completely as soon as they stop talking to themselves.

When mindfulness is focused on the process of thinking, an entirely different dimension of existence becomes visible. We see how our ridiculous, repetitive thought stream continually constructs our limited sense of self, through judgments, defences, ambitions, and compensations. Unexamined, we believe them. But if someone were to follow us close by and repeatedly whisper to us our own thoughts, we would quickly become bored with their words. If they continued, we would be dismayed by their constant criticisms and fears, then angry that they wouldn't ever shut up.

We might simply conclude that they were crazy. We do this to ourselves!

Stories have value. As an author, I have come to respect their evocative power, I share many stories and quotations daily. But even these stories are like fingers pointing to the moon. At best, they replace a deluded cultural narrative or a misleading tale with a tale of compassion. They touch us and lead us back to the mystery here and now.

Perhaps the most interesting intersection in the business world is between mindfulness and technology, as they appear to pull in opposite directions.

Stories do grab us. They take us in, transport us, and allow us to live vicariously and visually through another's experience. As I've said often in my work around presence, shared stories accelerate interpersonal connection. Learning to tell stories to capture, direct and sustain the attention of others is a key leadership skill. Storytelling also greatly helps anyone speaking or presenting in front of an audience.

As Steven Spielberg once said:

"The most amazing thing for me is that every single person who sees a movie, not necessarily one of my movies, brings a whole set of unique experiences. Now, through careful manipulation and good storytelling, you can get everybody to clap at the same time, to hopefully laugh at the same time, and to be afraid at the same time."

A Hopi American Indian proverb says: "Those who tell the stories rule the world." Well, just maybe these words of wisdom are totally correct.

It is true that in our information-saturated age, business leaders "will not be heard unless they're telling stories," says Nick Morgan, author of Power Cues and president and founder of Public Words, a communications consulting firm. "Facts and figures and all the rational things that we think are important in the business world actually do not stick in our minds at all," he says. But stories create 'sticky' memories by attaching emotions to things that happen. That means leaders who can create and share good stories have a powerful advantage over others. And fortunately, everyone has the ability to become a better storyteller. "We are programmed through our evolutionary biology to be both consumers and creators of story," says Jonah Sachs, CEO of Free Range Studios and author of Winning the Story Wars. "It certainly can be taught and learned."

Dan Ilett is the Managing Partner of Tollejo, a brand design and growth consultancy. Dan is considered the story and messaging architect connecting global experience in marketing, media and commercial leadership. Tollejo has created global brand strategy, advertising and client engagement campaigns for some of the largest companies in the world, leading marketing and commercial growth in FTSE and Fortune companies. And its journalists have covered stories for global media organisations. Dan discusses the choice abundance which drives a greater requirement for stories.

Consumers want to know they can trust a brand before they buy from it. But establishing that trust is a complex, convoluted journey that takes time. The customer has to know they're in safe hands – and that is getting harder for brands to manage.

The equation for trust was easier in pre-internet days. You would know the local shopkeeper or the brand in your town. You might have friends or family who worked there. And you almost certainly would read about them in the local paper from time to time. The community would tell stories about the brand – and that was enough.

But establishing trust on the internet with new brands or merchants was and still is different. Sure – the relevant online community will have reviews and publish stories of experiences about the brand. But as the abundance of product choice has skyrocketed, so has the requirement for better, more accurate stories and reviews to the point where, today, reviews have to be verified to ensure they are genuine.

Today some 97 per cent of consumers seek external validation of reviews from other internet sites before making a purchase, according to research company BIA/Kelsey. Yes, they check prices, but more often than not they want to know about the experience of others.

Mumsnet is the UK's largest internet forum for parents searching for answers and supplying recommendations. First launched in 2000, the forum has a reach of seven million unique visitors per month, successfully establishing its own brand – but posing big challenges for other brands. Forums like Mumsnet breed their own brand conversations. Brands can no longer take it for granted that they control conversations about them – but they also struggle to even engage with those forum conversations.

Still, stories go before purchases – so get involved in them. The story that goes before a brand interaction influences how much trust people will give. While great digital experience has been hailed as the holy grail for modern companies, consumers quickly become fed up with brands that fail to cater for unusual or bad user experiences. Typically these are experiences that don't fit the normal user journey, such as customer support, resolutions, payments or something else that is hard to scale.

For that reason, brands have realised that engagement is key to customers – not only the purchase and user experience as you'd expect – but also general behaviours and more recently, points of view on global affairs and news.

As this book is being written, the war in Ukraine rages on. Today's consumers understand that though they personally can do little to halt a tyrant like Putin, they can at least make it clear what they think of leaders like him and the decisions they make by moving away from a brand that does not demonstrate that it shares their disgust. They will even lobby for change on social media and call for boycotts on a whole range of issues including gender, race, equality, sustainability, police brutality … if a brand does not behave in a way they approve of. Brand trust drives share prices too. So global or listed brands have had to adapt far faster to social, news and customer pressures than ever before.

A survey by Brightlocal discovered that 91 per cent of millennials and young adults aged from 18 to 34 trust online reviews and personal recommendations to influence their purchase decisions. These recommendations offer customers a means to lower the risk of investment. The researchers, Arjun Chaudhuri and Morris B. Holbrook distinctly define brand trust as 'the willingness of consumers to rely on the ability of brands to perform their stated functions'.

But what are those stated functions? What are the promises they must live up to? Are they fulfilling their vision and purpose statements in the way consumers want it to be done?

The only way for global brands to operate today is to be honest, modern and act with integrity. Going back to our pre-internet analogy, not much was different in principle then. It is just that, now, brands must operate with more complexity, risk and the need to react to world affairs faster.

With every benefit of digitalisation, there is a risk. Some worry the internet has an overload of information; consumers sometimes have so many choices that choice overwhelms their purchase decisions. Worldwide, over 213 million companies offer a diverse array of services and products.

TED speaker Renata Salecl states that even after a sale is completed, the sense of excessive choice can trigger buyer's remorse in the most rational purchaser. So, as brands embrace new digital technologies for the scale they bring, they must also evolve to make sure engagement rules the day and they put people first.

In times of growing uncertainty, trust is built further when you demonstrate an ability to address unanticipated situations effectively and demonstrate a steady commitment to address the needs of all stakeholders in the best way possible.

The best business leaders begin by framing trust in economic terms for their companies. When an organization has low trust, the economic consequences can be huge. Everything will take longer and everything will cost more because the organization has to compensate for the lack of trust it commands. These costs can be quantified and when they are, leaders suddenly recognize that low trust is not merely a social issue. It becomes an economic matter. The dividends of high trust can also be calculated and this can help leaders make a compelling business case for trust.

The best leaders focus on making the creation of trust an explicit objective. Like any other goal, it must be measured and improved. It must be made clear to everyone that trust matters to management and leadership. The unambiguous message must be that this is the right thing to do and it is the right economic thing to do. One of the best ways to do this is to make an initial baseline measurement of organizational trust and then to track improvements over time.

It's clear from the news that the leaders of some of our most influential governments and corporations are making morally questionable decisions. These decisions will lose the trust of society, customers and employees. No amount of electronic communication – staff intranet, corporate social media, marketing emails – will fix this, yet many organizations assume this can replace meaningful dialogue even though this is the only real means of building trust and high-functioning relationships.

Finally, the true transformation starts with building credibility at the personal level. The foundation of trust is your own credibility, and it can be a real differentiator for any leader. A person's reputation is a direct reflection of their credibility and it precedes them in any interactions or negotiations they might have. When a leader's credibility and reputation are high, it enables them to establish trust quickly. Speed goes up, the cost goes down.

Mark F. Herbert

> *"Inside my empty bottle I was constructing a lighthouse*
> *while all the others were making ships."*
> Charles Simic

In my perspective, a *paradigm* is a particular belief system or model that we have adopted to give us a frame of reference.

Occasionally, and disappointingly, it is also the word used to justify a particular course of action.

In much of the Western world one paradigm that has been prevalent in business theory for well over 100 years is Scientific Management, formulated by industrial engineer Frederick W. Taylor. It has deep roots in the Calvinistic view that there are two kinds of people in the world: those who God favours and rewards with success, and the rest who are destined to toil at the direction of the blessed.

Taylor took that further, suggesting that the average person was inherently lazy and not very bright. In the interests of efficiency and social order, work should be broken down into steps that could be performed repetitively and efficiently by this average person. Managers would provide the thought and leadership; workers would just do what they were told and be grateful. The expression 'white collar worker' was coined by the thinkers who built on Taylor's assumptions in the 1920s and 1930s to describe those who say but don't do (and can therefore be sure their white shirts won't get dirty). Leaders don't perform tasks, they direct others to perform tasks.

Unfortunately, in many organizations this is still the prevalent thinking.

Dustin McKissen, founder and CEO of McKissen and Company, talked about this in his thought-provoking Inc Magazine blog post, *The rotten core of every MBA programme*. He specifically cites our ongoing infatuation with Frederick W. Taylor and the Scientific Management model.

"While Taylor's theories are viewed as harsh and impractical today, his work was still cited in every class I attended that discussed the roots of modern management science. What's not often discussed is how little

Taylor thought of the people who produced products in the factories he studied."

Traditional MBA programmes still train candidates to be what Lawrence Miller described as 'bureaucrats and administrators', in a book he published 30 years ago. Given that McKissen published his observations in 2016, I am quite disappointed at the lack of meaningful progress.

You can argue that I am wrong, that today's leaders are much more sensitive and empathetic and practice management differently, but I would say the results speak for themselves. Study after study continues to indicate that most aspiring managerial/ leadership candidates are pursuing that career path for primarily or exclusively financial reasons.,

If you look at our history, it was not that long ago that we accepted that royalty was divinely selected and that challenging royal authority was not just dangerous, but a crime against God. You can see, then, why Scientific Management was and remains compelling for some.

There are just a couple of problems.

- The new generations don't buy into it, and they represent the future workforce
- Even before the global pandemic, businesses and organizations struggled to attract and retain the talent they needed to execute their organizational plans and objectives

When I decided to write my first book, there was rather a lot going on in my life: I had just left a job I was very invested in and it had been one of the few times in my career when I worked for an organization that allowed me to put into practice some of the management and leadership concepts I had pondered for a very long time, enabling me to determine whether or not they were viable in the real world.

My departure was bittersweet. Although we had managed to achieve a lot, both strategically and in how we interacted with our communities and our employees, I didn't always show the patience and consideration my colleagues and boss deserved. Unfortunately, when I get tired or overly invested, I can develop sharp edges and become self-destructive, and I am sure both traits were visible during those last few months. I hope with this new book to share some of my experiences and some of what I have learned in the intervening thirteen years since that first book. Some of the things that we hope to share now weren't on my radar back then. Had they been, it's likely they would have saved me, my clients, and employees some pain and suffering.

Our intent in this book is to explore the reasons we find ourselves in this place and what we should consider changing if we don't want to continue along the path we are on.

Exactly as I publish my blog posts and make my presentations, I don't position myself as the expert; I am a practitioner who has made almost all of the mistakes that I mention, and an idealist who hopes we can all embrace a different way. At this stage of my career I aspire to build lighthouses, beacons that illuminate the potential rocks and shoals, and not turn-by-turn GPS-style directions and instructions. I am not an academic. Much of what is I have to say is anecdotal; I don't have an extensive bibliography and lots of charts and graphs. Again, that is by intent.

I hope that readers will be able to take away a small measure of value and that, one person at a time, we can begin to embrace a different business model that focuses on managing whole people.

PART 1

Communication

Control is not leadership!

Saying won't make it so. Listening is as vital to good communication as telling it how it is – perhaps more so. Then act on what you are told – 'you said, we did' is how your people know you heard. Delivery of the message is no proof that it was received – check understanding. Companies that survived the enforced isolation and fragmentation of the long pandemic and even, in some cases, emerged in even better shape were those that placed a premium on building trust and genuine buy-in. You want the people around you to trust you, and to work intelligently and with commitment?

Explain what's going on – and why.

CHAPTER ONE

The broken road: travelling from processes to relationships

"In organizations, real power and energy is generated through relationships. The patterns of relationships and the capacity to form them are more important than tasks, functions, roles, and positions."

Margaret Wheatley

I like using metaphors both for my own edification and as a way of illustrating a concept for others. It may be that only I see the connection, but I hope not.

One of my favourite pieces of music is a tune taken to number one by Rascal Flatts a few years back. 'The Broken Road' describes a personal journey the singer takes before meeting his life partner. As I look back at my own broken road, I find the metaphor a useful tool to set the stage for sharing my thoughts.

A few years ago, my brother and I had the opportunity to join a couple in a round of golf. I was a little taken aback when the husband took me aside and asked me to be patient; his wife was suffering stage four terminal brain cancer that impaired her vision. Sometimes he needed to get her set up correctly to make her shots. The following four hours or so was a lesson in life and in golf.

She was one of the most gracious and positive people I have met in a very long time. She also had a wonderful, consistent approach to her golf game, never overpowering the ball or her stroke. Unlike the rest of us she took a shortcut, (humor intended), and played exclusively the fairway and the greens on her way to the ball.

I once had an opportunity to work intimately with a client who is involved in the health care sector. His role is on the philanthropic side of the organization rather than the operational or caregiving side. With the squeeze in health care delivery in the US, philanthropy is increasingly important, especially in the not-for-profit sector where health care providers are trying to make up for the shortfalls created by the number of Americans who have lost the coverage they once had from their employer or the government. Providers are also trying to anticipate any further growth in the uninsured under Obamacare. (For the record, I don't think Obamacare created more uninsured; I think in fact it tries to address current issues in our health care delivery system that are not being addressed today, but that is a different topic for a different day.)

I think we do have a broken road with our health care system. We manage delivery of health care rather than health, and that means we focus on the system rather than addressing the problem. I also think the road is broken in terms of how we are trying to address other issues and concerns, especially the interdependence of sectors of society and people.

I began my professional career in human resources over four decades ago. It struck me then how much of the infrastructure and tactics of that discipline were based on processes and transactions rather than relationships. Things have changed much over those three decades: we have gone through several title changes, from Personnel to Employee Relations and from there to Human Resources, but the fundamental premise has also changed significantly.

A current buzzword, and the one that is increasingly usurping the notion of Human Resources, is 'Human Capital'. I don't debate that the combined talents, knowledge, and abilities of our workforce come together to create an important asset for our organizations and must be aligned to its purpose and managed and measured, but that is not the output. The output is provided by people.

I personally despise the term and concept of "human capital". In my mind it diminishes people to an asset or entry on the balance sheet, a significant pivot in the wrong direction.

My personal broken road has clearly established that for me.

For the last thirty years or so I have been attempting to promulgate the concept of employee engagement and the alignment of individual and organizational goals. It has been validating over the last five years or so to see literature and discussions recognizing that this concept and process may be the most significant key to organizational performance and sustainability available to us. Organizations that successfully develop and implement true engagement enjoy competitive advantages in every key performance indicator that the financial and other markets like to track. The literature is replete with examples. The foundation for engagement, at least in my mind, is based on two fundamental concepts – trust and congruency.

I think that Stephen M.R. Covey does a super nice job of describing the elements of trust in his book, *The Speed of Trust.*

He talks about trust being built on a foundation of two primary pillars:

- credibility
- behaviour

Credibility is based on some critical sub-factors including character – as expressed through your integrity and congruency (perceived shared values) – and your competence – in the form of your demonstrated capabilities and results. The key is that these need to be integrated and in sync. Character without competence doesn't create credibility and neither does competence without character. You must do both.

Behaviour speaks to who you are, not what you say. It's about how you act or demonstrate those behaviours. Covey identifies thirteen key behaviours. I won't go into all of them, but some key behaviours include qualities such as: clear expectations, the extension of trust, practising personal and professional accountability, and straight talk. He and I also believe that the ability to build and facilitate trust is a learnable skill; it isn't something you are born with or without.

The dividends of trust are huge. They can be measured in every key performance indicator from profitability to retention and productivity. You are going to hear a lot more about the model developed by Covey Junior (a term I use to distinguish Stephen MR Covey from his father, Stephen Covey, author of the famous Seven Habits series) in the upcoming pages. I have not found too many other places where trust is described so simply and elegantly.

Similarly, Ron Willingham in designing his *Integrity Selling*

System™ discusses the concept of congruency at some length. He provides a model for creating congruency or alignment based on five factors:

- Our view of the activity (do we see it as worthwhile or repugnant?)
- Our view of our ability to do the activity (perceived competency)
- The relationship between the activity and our personal values
- Our commitment to do the 'work'
- Our belief in the product, service, and mission (organizational value proposition)

Ron indicates – and I agree – that if there is a lack of congruence or alignment with any of those things, then sustained excellent performance is unlikely.

It is really striking that traditional training and reward theory address only the competency and, maybe if we are lucky, the 'commitment to the work' because of perceived extrinsic and intrinsic motivators. That leaves three out of the five unaccounted for and doesn't seem like a recipe for success – at least not on a sustained level.

Those other three are those pesky 'people-ey' soft skills and the relationship-type stuff.

In my mind, where we go from here represents a broken road. We can learn from all that has gone before and embrace new solutions, engaging and aligning people not just in our 'work' relationships but also creating a new model for how we work together and how different elements of our society interact together. Or we can ignore it. I don't think our current models of trickle-down economics and compliance-based methodologies, or our process-based solutions address either the trust or congruency gaps. We need a new model.

So, I guess each of us will have to determine where this broken road takes us.

My metaphor is perhaps too esoteric. If you find it so, I hope you at least enjoy the music.

CHAPTER TWO

Control is not leadership

"Being a leader changes everything. Before you are a leader, success is all about you. It's about your performance, your contributions. It's about getting called upon and having the right answers. When you become a leader, success is all about growing others. Your success as a leader comes not from what you do but from the reflected glory of the people you lead."

Jack Welch, former CEO of General Electric

Over the last few years, I have written and spoken on a variety of topics that largely share a common theme: our current employment model must be repaired, if not completely overhauled.

As a society, we bailed out the financial services industry after the disastrous 2007-2008 crash in the markets, but we are seeing very little short-term return on investment and most of the banks still aren't lending.

We bailed out the automotive industry as well. Although they have mostly returned to profitability, there are still those who argue that supporting them was a flawed strategy, inconsistent with our economic model and with the intent of the Founding Fathers when they framed the Constitution. I disagree with the former position (and wasn't there for the latter).

We are at the culmination of several key events and identifying the issues they have raised and resolving them will be critical to creating a lasting solution. Our biggest issues are:

- Somewhere in the process of moving from an agrarian society to an industrial society, we gave up much of the founding principle of personal competency.
- We have not captured the energy and commitment of the American worker. In many cases, we have used technology and systems against people rather than on their behalf. In short, we have disengaged them.
- Our management and leadership models do not appropriately value and reinforce the importance of relationships and people.

I look at my hometown community and in some ways, I see what is happening there as a microcosm of what is happening across the country and even internationally.

My hometown grew up out of the extraction industry and the railroads. We harvested timber and aggregates and shipped them all over the world. The families who benefited from those businesses invested in their community. We have a world-class university, a world-class performing arts centre, and at one time I believe we had one of the best K-12 education systems in the country.

We have world-class quality of life as well. Within minutes of our community, you can snow ski, visit the ocean, raft world-class rapids, enjoy incredible fishing and many other outdoor activities. If you make a reasonable wage, it is also an affordable community. Those are the things that brought me here more than twenty years ago.

We also have significant issues. A few years ago, the combination of environmental restrictions and technology began to limit our extraction-based economy. I combine the two factors because my understanding is that even if we were to release thousands of acres back into production, technology exists today to extract their natural resources with a much smaller workforce.

Like much of the U.S. Northwest, we accepted an economy that was, to a large extent, based on a kind of governmental co-dependency. We receive millions in lieu of the revenues we would have seen in harvesting the timber. The issue is that the subsidy was intended to be temporary, and we did not execute solid plans to replace those revenues with family-wage jobs. The subsidies have been extended year to year in smaller and smaller amounts.

Now our affordability – the cost of housing as it relates to the wage base – is one of the lowest in the country. Our public safety infrastructure is at a low point; the number of sworn police officers per capita is one of the lowest in the nation for a community our size. We release criminals because we don't have appropriate infrastructure to incarcerate them – we lack enough police officers to arrest them or sufficient prosecutors to arraign them.

For what we define as 'livability', we have made decisions to restrict the supply and use of land for industrial purposes. That has further eroded our ability to attract and retain businesses. As taxpayers we decided to limit the market valuation of real

11

estate and, although it made us attractive to retirees and others on a fixed income, it reduced the tax base as well. Combined, a limited number of industrial taxpayers and capped real estate taxes have created kind of a negative perfect storm. Our lack of planning has reached critical mass.

What has happened in my community is not unique. I use it as an illustration to make my point.

Personal competency, like personal property, was one of the concepts embedded in the original Bill of Rights as written by our Founding Fathers. It was the idea that in America, you could reinvent yourself; you were not bound by your heritage. You had the right and the responsibility to make decisions about your future and to ensure your economic welfare and that of your family.

At one time, we represented the best place in the world to do that. We had unlimited frontiers. When we saw crowding or other issues, we opened additional land supply and 'homesteaders' were welcome to pursue property ownership and the American dream. Then, during the late 1800s and early 1900s, two changes halted that. The first was that we ran out of frontiers; the second was our move from an agrarian to an industrial economy.

Franklin D. Roosevelt talked about that in his original Presidential campaign. FDR, as he became universally known, described how industrialization combined with the loss of frontiers created a new feudalism. The advent of corporations as legal persons, and the concessions granted to industrialists who built the railroads and other infrastructure had created wealth and power that most royalty would envy. Industrial 'serfs' were the people who populated the factories. We often forget that until 1934 there was no legal right for employees to collectively bargain with employers. Trickle-down economics weren't trickling down.

Meanwhile, some of the actions taken by Roosevelt as part of his New Deal were seen at that time as the worst kind of socialism.

Although he didn't necessarily intend it, I think that much of the infrastructure created during and shortly after the New Deal contributed to the loss of personal competency. Most employees grew to expect their employer to 'take care of them'. The New Deal's wage and price freezes created innovative solutions at the bargaining table. Things like employer-provided retirement, health care, shortened work weeks and other welfare benefits became commonplace. As we were the dominant economy emerging from World War II, we just passed a lot of these costs along. We owned or controlled most of the industrial capacity of the world.

We further gave up personal competency when we got sloppy. We let the quality of our products and services slip because of our control of the markets. Many of us forget that people like Edward Deming were talking about total quality and his own form of empowerment in the late 1940s. In its own way, the total quality movement has some of the same underpinnings as personal competency. We rejected it because we didn't have to be any better – we owned the market.

Similarly, we didn't invest in new production capacity and techniques because we still controlled the market. Then, when products from Asia and Europe began coming into our markets and were embraced by American consumers, we passed trade tariffs rather than looking at root causes like quality and production costs. We eventually ceded whole segments to foreign corporations and became a service economy.

The next thing was that we offshored. We moved production capacity to other locations where the regulatory environment was less rigorous and cost of labour was much cheaper, again rather than exploring root causes.

Somewhere in this process, there was another perfect storm when technology met health care. The innovations over the last fifty years in health care are amazing, ranging from 'miracle drugs' to new technology that prolong both the length and quality of life. It is also very expensive. The responsibility for 'picking up the tab' has rested with large employers and the government. In about the mid-1980s, the costs of these programmes showed up on the radar of employers. In most cases, rather than once again exploring root causes, our approach was to cost shift.

As a society we still have the mentality that embraces I should be able to eat and drink what I want, refuse to exercise and abuse my health, and then some combination of my employer and the government should pay for it. The outcome is that in the United States we spend a significantly greater proportion of our GDP on delivering health care than any other industrialized country. Yet we have mediocre results on indicators such as morbidity, mortality, and other measurements of key health care outcomes.

Then the social contract expired. Employers began embracing defined contributions rather than defined benefit programmes in retirement and health care. We moved production offshore to reduce costs and had no U.S.-based employees to take care of. Companies that had never reduced their workforces or cut benefits found out it wasn't that bad. For the first time in generations, we saw the standard of living reduce rather than improve.

Disengaging the workforce

I remember my surprise when I entered the workforce and discovered that we didn't think employees were very smart. We relied heavily on compliance-based models rather than explaining our goals and enlisting their support. We rarely involved employees in decisions about how to do something. We didn't explain systems like health care or materials management or, in some cases, even the legal environment. Managers managed and people did. I was naïve and wondered why, if we thought all these people were stupid, did we hire them? I got some opportunities to test some of my theories and found out I wasn't entirely wrong.

I remember being in graduate school and attending a presentation by a Fortune 100 organization about implementing their company-wide approach to total quality. I asked them how they were working with the leadership of their collective bargaining units to implement the plan. They looked at me like I was insane and informed me that this was a 'company' programme, and they had no intention of partnering with the union. I later heard they never really managed to implement the initiative with the degree of success they imagined.

A comparative study on collective bargaining, which compares the U.S. with European and Asian approaches to the introduction of technology, reveals that in Europe and Japan, unions participate in decisions about the selection and deployment of technology. In the U.S., employers are legally bound to negotiate the impact or effects of technology, but this is a reactive rather than a proactive approach. I don't begrudge the autoworkers and others the benefit of a fair living wage, but we all recognize that the 'protections' built into many contracts have created much of the financial difficulty being faced by the big three automakers.

Let's be honest: when we are evaluating a new system or capital purchase, how often is the number of full-time equivalent jobs it will replace a major consideration? As Americans we embrace technology. When I look at the attention and time we lavish on the selection of a piece of technology versus the time and energy we put into our recruitment and selection processes, the irony stuns me. Rarely do I see an organization where executives in human resources are regarded with the same esteem as technical staff.

The studies on employee and customer engagement came to some conclusions that will make many executives cringe. For instance, the foundations of engagement are based on trust, communications, and shared values; there is no 'system' or software that can recoup that $200 billion. You must work with people.

The importance of relationships

As alluded to in the previous section, engagement with both employees and customers is about relationship. It is about trust and shared values. It is also about respect, which goes back to the concept of personal competency.

My colleague Ty Warren, in his book *White Hat Leadership,* talks about how what we call 'soft skills' aren't soft at all. Creating and communicating a vision that people share and commit to is not a soft skill. We have a fascination with leadership.

Marcus Buckingham says that the most important role of a leader is creating clarity. Richard Rumelt of UCLA's Anderson School of Management takes a similar position. He says the job of management and leadership is to remove ambiguity for our employees, to give context to their tasks and responsibilities as it relates to the overall purpose. Do those sound-like soft skills to you?

So let's look at the curriculum of the average MBA programme. The proportion devoted to communications, setting expectations, and skills, such as coaching or giving and receiving constructive feedback, is dwarfed by modules that cover financial modelling, economic models, and other related studies.

Ty differentiates explorers and mappers: explorers are the visionaries and risk takers, the entrepreneurs, and those skills, he argues, are transitional. Once the enterprise is up and going, you need capable administrators and managers. Our business education model is highly biased towards 'mapping' skills. Mapping skills rely heavily on the old Taylor mentality of steps, instruction, and rote following that diminish individual thought.

That works if the system is working. The observation from the AMA I mentioned earlier is worth repeating here: the modern workplace is sadly lacking in collaborative, communication, and creative skills.

We need a new model!

We need to bring personal competency back into our society. Employers will not be able to fund the health care model and individuals need to accept personal responsibility for participating in decisions about their health, their careers, and their retirement. That is what the Founding Fathers intended. On the other hand, we live in a global economy. What happens in Shanghai or Saigon effects what happens in Sheboygan. We don't have any real physical frontiers to conquer. So:

17

- We need to be open to models which represent public/private partnership
- We need to fix our education and health care infrastructure
- We need to rebuild our economic base

While we don't have a physical frontier, we can reclaim the $200 billion we are losing to presenteeism. We can develop and implement systems to engage the 70 per cent of workers who are not engaged and enjoy those productivity and sustainability improvements. We can fix the root causes.

My experience and my research say that the way you create engagement is by starting with trust. Engagement is for and about people, and about alignment between individual and organizational goals.

CHAPTER THREE

Trust: what creates it, what builds it

> *"The leaders who work most effectively, it seems to me, never say 'I.' And that's not because they have trained themselves not to say 'I.' They don't think 'I.' They think 'we'; they think 'team.' They understand their job to be to make the team function. They accept responsibility and don't sidestep it, but 'we' gets the credit.... This is what creates trust, what enables you to get the task done."*
>
> Peter Drucker, author of *Managing for the Future*

Since I wrote my last book, I've had the opportunity to read some great work. I would put Stephen M.R. Covey's *The Speed of Trust* close to the top of that list. He is the son of leadership guru Stephen Richards Covey. Perhaps I am biased, but I find his work much more compelling than that of his late father. He points up some ideas that really speak to me. Every organization, he says, either earns a trust dividend or pays a trust tax. Really well-managed organizations make that choice cognitively; others have it 'happen' to them.

Trust is among those interesting words, like empathy and

integrity, that embody an important concept but which, I think, make people feel uncomfortable.

As Covey Junior further explores the notion of trust, he argues that it sits on a 'foundation' of two primary pillars, **credibility, and behaviour**; and that the credibility pillar rests on the 'pilings' of **character and competence**.

Covey further **breaks down character**, describing it as being **a function of integrity and perceived intent**. So, he says, integrity is when you say what you are going to do – and then do it. In other words, are you congruent with your stated values? Intent, meanwhile, comes down to whether you play win-win or win-lose. Certainly, integrity is important to me. Finally, Covey argues that his second underpinning factor for true credibility, **competence**, is **composed of capability and results**.

He says – and I agree – that you can't be credible if you fail to deliver in both character and competence. Character without being able to deliver is nice but doesn't get the job done. Capability without character justifies our actions without taking others into account.

Returning to Covey's two primary pillars, we now turn to behavior. **Behaviour is who you are**, **and this is determined by how you act**.

- Do you give and extend trust?
- Do you demonstrate and practice personal accountability?
- Do you set clear expectations?
- Do you practice transparency?

What I like about the way that Covey describes trust is that it isn't blind trust. There is reciprocity and expectations between the parties. There is also experience and information. It is a process or journey rather than an event.

He moves on from this detailed analysis of trust's foundations to describe the three distinct levels that arise from them: **deterrence, knowledge (or competence) and identity.**

Deterrence is the model that formed much of our early societal relationships, and it is still alive and well today. There was a time when the nobility and wealthy believed they had an absolute entitlement to be trusted because of their power and social position. Even today, most human resources executives will tell you that the most important role they fulfil for their employers is ensuring compliance which, to me at least, is a kind of deterrence.

Knowledge or competence, Covey tells us, is a form of trust often based on credentials. This is a type of trust I think we have over-invested in. If we think back to Frederick W. Taylor's *Scientific Management*, its core assumption is that 'superior' white-collar leaders direct the behaviour of human drones who can't be trusted to make good decisions on their own. I look at some of my experiences as a change agent, human resources executive, and consultant over the last forty years and I see where some things went very well on this basis, and where some things went very wrong. Many of our 'system interventions' are all about competence. They are very transactional and functional. We certify, license, and apply all kinds of 'objective' measures.

Yet we leave out relationships. We have proliferated the idea that certifications and degree programmes give someone an entitlement to be trusted and respected. I see this very commonly among new graduates of the MBA programmes that have become ubiquitous in industry. Typically, the new graduate assumes entitlement to a leadership role even though very little of most MBA curricula focuses on managing relationships.

I see a lot of human resource professionals pursuing Six Sigma or other coaching accreditations which teach great skills but don't guarantee that students will emerge with relationship-building abilities. The fact is that the legal infrastructure that guides interactions between employee and employer in our country is based upon mistrust. It is incredibly byzantine and adversarial. It almost assumes a lack of character and positive intent. I am not naïve – I know the history – but take a close look: much of the work of HR professionals is now about compliance with the myriad of rules and regulations that codify mistrust.

Let's turn finally to **identity**, Covey's third level of trust. Based on the twin elements of personal experiences and credibility, it is earned over time and in Covey's opinion – and mine – is essential to long-term high-functioning relationships, whether personal or professional. This is trust based on real transparency and intimacy.

To bring all this together, let me now draw your attention to two things we know for sure.

- **When organizations invest in trust, recent studies have shown that they see significant benefit to every key performance indicator** if they do this through cultivating strong employment brands and true engagement models built in large part upon the foundation that Covey describes.
- The research also shows that **those initiatives fail if they are not founded on trust.**

Some of the factors that support and enhance trust-based models include:

- Alignment with organizational values
- Clear management expectations and feedback
- Clear internal communications about organizational initiatives and alignment with values and goals
- Positive, compelling work environment

What diminishes trust?

- Lack of autonomy in work tasks
- Poor relationships with peers and co-workers
- Workplace culture disconnected with organizational values and mission
- Poor management skills

These factors lead to lower engagement, higher turnover and lousy results.

It's important to Millennials and Gen Xers, who will soon represent much of the workforce, that they get plenty of the first set of factors and none of the second. And they aren't going to change to accommodate us.

CHAPTER FOUR

Lead with TI – trust intelligence

*"Sometimes it is said that man cannot be trusted with
the government of himself. Can he, then, be trusted with
the government of others? Or have we found angels in
the form of kings to govern him? Let history answer this
question."*

Thomas Jefferson, 3rd President of the United States

The global pandemic, triggered by Covid-19, presented the world with the ultimate test of leadership across industries and geographies. From health care to government, school systems to non-profits, almost every organization has experienced unprecedented challenges that have tested the values and skills of its leaders. Navigating this uncertainty requires mental and emotional stamina, courage and compassion.

The balance between IQ and emotional intelligence is a topic I've addressed in a number of blog posts: *Why emotional intelligence is leadership, team spirit and company culture; Emotional intelligence and your survival through the fourth industrial revolution;* and, more recently, *The four intelligences; IQ, EI, SI, DI and why we need Wisdom Intelligence (WI).*

It is often debated that the importance of different types of intelligence. I have tried to explain the four intelligences, to explain why we and our fellow humans need to balance skill, competence and moral and ethical behaviours to be truly effective in this new world. And while there are just a few elemental forces that hold our world together, the glue of society is trust. This leads me to discussion of a fifth kind of intelligence – TI, or 'trust intelligence'.

I once quoted: "The importance of trust, integrity and experience has always been critical at IBEM. In my experience, this is ethically and morally important, but it is also our business mantra."

No less a person than his Holiness the Dalai Lama once said: "To earn trust, money and power aren't enough; you have to show some concern for others. You can't buy trust in the supermarket."

Trust in a leader allows organizations and communities to flourish, while the absence of trust can cause fragmentation, conflict and even war. That's why we need to trust our leaders, our family members, our friends and our co-workers, albeit in different ways.

Trust is hard to define, but we do know when it's lost. When that happens, we withdraw our energy and level of engagement. We go on an internal strike, not wanting to be sympathetic to the person who we feel has hurt us or treated us wrongly. We may not show it outwardly, but we are less likely to tell the formerly trusted person that we are upset, to share what is important to us or to follow through on commitments. As a result, we pull back from that person and no longer feel part of their world. This loss of trust can be obvious or it can be somewhat hidden, especially if we pretend to be present but inwardly disengage. Those who have done something to lose our trust may not even know it.

On the positive side, trust makes people feel eager to be part of a relationship or group with a shared purpose and have a willingness to depend on each other. When trust is intact, we will willingly contribute what is needed, not just by offering our presence, but also by sharing our dedication, talent, energy and honest thoughts on how the relationship or group is working.

The dynamics of trust are delicate in important relationships, and the loss of trust can be costly — not only psychologically, but also financially and in terms of work and livelihood. What's helpful to remember is that trust is an ongoing exchange between people and is not static. Trust can be earned. It can be lost. And it can be regained.

Trust is the new disruptor, one that businesses must master to realize the full power of data and new intelligent technologies.

Markets face complex and accelerating change. This is fuelled by intelligent technologies such as robotic process automation and the artificial intelligence that has given us speech recognition, natural language processing and computer vision, based on machine-learning algorithms and enabled by limitless cloud-based computing capacity.

The proliferation of inexpensive sensor technology has generated massive amounts of data. Artificial intelligence consumes it to 'learn', make decisions, and deliver enhanced insights. But can this intelligence be trusted?

While those able to exploit how new intelligent technologies use data are gaining competitive advantages, they also face a new set of risks. For some, the mode and speed at which intelligent technologies digest and act on data is creating unexpected outcomes, for instance, fracturing trust with customers, markets and across ecosystems. Would you use online banking if a massive data breach had broken your trust with that bank or, perhaps, all banks? Do you have enough trust to get into a self-driving car?

So a key question for executives has emerged: can you trust the intelligence driving your enterprise?

We are living in a time of increasingly intelligent technologies. It is also a time when an organization's ability to be trusted really matters. The way data and intelligent technologies are being used is creating significant trust gaps. The benchmark 2020 Edelman Trust Barometer told us that the public feels intelligent technology is moving too fast and that regulators can't keep up.

Plenty of high-profile examples of data misuse and unintended consequences from the use of AI have contributed to these gaps. Take, for instance, the moment when an AI tool decided to reconstruct an image of Barack Obama to turn him into a white man. The hot debate in the AI community was whether the AI programme's learning had embedded a bias towards creating more photos of white people than people of colour. Was this the result of incomplete data or indicative of racial bias baked into AI from non-diverse data sets and development teams?

Trust gaps have reframed the question of 'can tech do this?' into 'should tech do this?' It's no longer about capabilities. It's about trust in the intelligence that a business uses, and on which customers, markets, regulators and ecosystems rely. Can companies and government organizations be sure what outcomes their technologies will produce? Do they have reliable methods for identifying, tracing and correcting unintended outcomes?

Without trust, the ability of an organization to operate and innovate is reduced and slowed down.

In low-trust environments, you'll see low morale, disengagement and a lack of commitment. You'll also see people manipulating, distorting facts and withholding information. There will be resistance to new ideas, the proliferation of blame culture, finger-pointing, overpromising, under-delivering and, often, tension and fear. Everything will take longer to do and everything will cost more.

The converse in high trust cultures is equally true. When the trust goes up in an organization, the speed will go up and costs will come down. Your ability to collaborate goes up, as does your ability to attract, retain and engage people. When trust goes up, you'll see people sharing information, unafraid to make mistakes, being more creative, more willing to be accountable and working with greater energy and satisfaction. When you move the needle on trust, you move all kinds of other needles with it.

So, as businesses and governments transform to meet new challenges, it's essential to embed TI into the core of their operations.

Enterprises powered by trust will be able to deliver on all three transformation drivers: people, technology and innovation. They'll be able to leapfrog their competitors; to shape new markets; to lead into better futures.

It's hard to quantify exactly how important trust is for a business. For business owners, a lack of trust is the biggest expense. It may take years for a manager or an executive to develop the trust of their employees, but only moments to lose it. Without trust, transactions cannot occur, influence is destroyed, leaders can lose teams and salespeople can lose sales. The list goes on. Trust and relationships, much more than money, are the currency of business.

Trust is the natural result of thousands of tiny actions, words, thoughts, and intentions. Trust does not happen all at once; gaining trust takes work. It might take years of calling on a certain client to break through and fully gain their comfort and trust. Yet despite the importance of trust in the business world today, few leaders have given it the focus and nurturing it deserves.

Business strategist and author David Horsager speaks internationally on the bottom-line impact of trust. He has developed a system with which he teaches leaders how to build the *Eight Pillars of Trust*:

- Clarity – People trust the clear and mistrust the ambiguous
- Compassion – People put faith in those who care beyond themselves
- Character – People notice those who do what is right over what is easy
- Competency – People have confidence in those who stay fresh, relevant, and capable
- Commitment – People believe in those who stand firm through adversity
- Connection – People want to follow, buy from, and be around friends
- Contribution – People immediately respond to results
- Consistency – People love to see the little things done consistently

Finally, it is crucial to understand that trust is fundamental to genuine success of any kind be that the trust you have with your team, colleagues or family. Traditionally, businesses have relied on 'command and control', focusing on rigid hierarchies and compliance from employees. We must shift from 'command and control' to a 'trust and inspire' leadership model.

Trusting and inspiring your team is defined by commitment from both sides, with a focus on effectiveness and fostering a growth mindset. It is based on the belief that employees are creative, collaborative, and full of potential. Through trust, you can inspire them to do their best work.

CHAPTER FIVE

Why our real connections are disappearing

"Cell phones, mobile email, and all the other cool and slick gadgets can cause massive losses in our creative output and overall productivity."

Robin S. Sharma

In January 2019, I wrote a blog, *Are we too busy to connect to real people?* and it had more significant views than any other I have ever posted in the last seven years – and there have been a few: 560 blogs in all.

Some alarming statistics, combined with my own interest in human connection and mental health awareness, had led me to ask a question that obviously touched many other people. I was clearly not alone in thinking that we all should start to understand the need for more human-to-human interaction and fulfilment from others, our work, our loved ones, our friends and, importantly, why we should make time for each other.

A decade ago, smart devices promised to change the way we think and interact, and they have – but not by making us smarter. Here I explore the growing body of scientific evidence that suggests digital distraction is damaging our minds.

Today, it is estimated that more than five billion people have mobile devices and over half of these connections are smartphones. It's changing the way we do countless things, from taking photos to summoning taxis.

A recent report from Hitachi Vantara in collaboration with MIT, *From innovation to monetization: The economics of data-driven transformation*, cites the exponential growth in big data arising from the multiplicity of data sources that range from sensors, edge devices and other connected hardware. It quotes expert estimates that 2.5 quintillion bytes of data are generated every day and had piled up to over 44 trillion gigabytes by 2020.

A statement from global market intelligence researchers IDC on the same subject: "150 billion systems and devices will be connected across the globe by 2025."

Smartphones have also changed both our behaviour and our culture. They have changed our natures in elemental ways, reshaping the way we think and interact. For all the many conveniences they bring, they have changed not just industries or habits but people themselves.

The evidence for this comes from psychiatrists, neuroscientists, marketers and public health experts. What these people say – and what their research shows – is that smartphones are causing real damage to our minds and relationships and this is measurable in seconds shaved off the average attention span, reduced brain power, declines in work-life balance and fewer hours of family and friends time.

They have impaired our ability to remember. They make it more difficult to daydream and think creatively. They make us more vulnerable to anxiety. They make parents ignore their children. And they are, to all intents and purposes, addictive, if not perhaps in the contested clinical sense.

Consider this: in the first five years of the smartphone era, the proportion of internet and app users who said internet use interfered with their family time nearly tripled, rising from 11 per cent to 28 per cent. And this: smartphone use takes about the same cognitive toll as losing a full night's sleep. In other words, they are making us worse at being alone and worse at being together.

Ten years into the smartphone experiment, we may be reaching a tipping point. Made wary by the mounting evidence, smartphone users are beginning to recognize the downside of the convenient little mini-computer we keep pressed against our thigh or cradled in our palm and buzzing on our bedside table while we sleep.

The projected speed of 5G mobile networks is breathtaking. Simply said, 5G is widely believed to be smarter, faster and more efficient than 4G, promising mobile data speeds that far outstrip the fastest home broadband network currently available to consumers. With speeds of up to 100 gigabits per second, 5G is set to be perhaps 100 times faster than 4G. How will this affect us humans?

More recently, researchers who study the relationship of mobile phone use and mental health have also found that excessive or 'maladaptive' use of our phones may be leading to greater incidences of depression and anxiety in users. In its regularly updated mental health statistics, the Mental Health Foundation England reveals that in England:

- 1 in 4 people experience mental health issues each year
- 676 million people are affected by mental health issues worldwide

- At any given time, 1 in 6 working-age adults have symptoms associated with mental ill health
- Mental health illness is the largest single source of burden of disease in the UK. Mental health illnesses are more common, long-lasting and impactful than other health conditions
- Mental ill health is responsible for 72 million working days lost and costs £34.9 billion each year – but different studies estimate the cost of mental ill health in different ways and other reputable research estimates costs as high as £74–£99 billion a year
- The total cost of mental ill health in England is estimated at £105 billion per year

Nowhere is the dawning awareness of the problem with smartphones more acute than in the Californian idylls that created them. In recent years ex-employees of Google, Apple and Facebook, including former top executives, have begun to raise the alarm about smartphones and social media apps, warning especially of their effects on children.

Chris Marcellino, who helped develop the iPhone's push notifications at Apple, told The Guardian newspaper that smartphones hook people using the same neural pathways as gambling and drugs.

Sean Parker, ex-president of Facebook, recently admitted that the world-bestriding social media platform was designed to hook users with spurts of dopamine, a complicated neurotransmitter released when the brain expects a reward or accrues fresh knowledge. "You're exploiting a vulnerability in human psychology," he said. "[The inventors] understood this, consciously, and we did it anyway."

Peddling this addiction made Mr. Parker and his tech-world colleagues absurdly rich. At the time of writing, Facebook is valued at a little more than half a trillion dollars. Global revenue from smartphone sales reached $435 billion (U.S.) in 2020.

Now, some of the early executives of these tech firms look on their success as tainted.

At a public talk in November, Chamath Palihapitiya, former vice-president of use growth at Facebook, drew a hushed audience at Stanford business school as he said:

"I feel tremendous guilt. I think we all knew in the back of our minds… something bad could happen. The short-term, dopamine-driven feedback loops that we have created are destroying how society works. They are eroding the core foundations of how people behave."

Business leaders are grappling with the issue, too. Bank of England analyst Dan Nixon argues that the distraction wrought by smartphones may be hurting productivity. It takes office workers an average of 25 minutes to get back on task after an interruption, he notes, while workers who are habitually interrupted by email become likelier to 'self-interrupt' with little procrastination breaks.

If we have lost control over our relationship with smartphones, it is by design. In fact, the business model of the devices demands it. Because most popular websites and apps don't charge for access, the internet is financially sustained by eyeballs. That is, the longer and more often you spend staring at Facebook or Google, the more money they can charge advertisers.

To ensure that our eyes remain firmly glued to our screens, the internet giants have become our little virtuosos of persuasion, cajoling us into checking our smartphones – and the digital worlds they connect us to – again and again, and for longer than we intend.

On some level, we do know that smartphones are designed to be addictive. The way we talk about them is steeped in the language of dependence, albeit playfully: the CrackBerry, the Instagram fix, the Angry Bird binge. But the best minds who have studied these devices are saying it's not really a joke.

Consider the effect smartphones have on our ability to focus.

John Ratey, an associate professor of psychiatry at Harvard Medical School and an expert on attention deficit disorder (ADD), has said the problem is actually getting worse: "We're not developing the attention muscles in our brain nearly as much as we used to," he said. In fact, Professor Ratey has noticed a convergence between his ADD patients and the rest of the world. The behaviour of people with ADD and people with smartphones are 'absolutely the same', he says.

It is widely known that Chinese middle-schoolers found something similar. Among more than 7,000 students, mobile phone ownership was found to be 'significantly associated' with levels of inattention more usually seen in people with attention deficit disorder.

Maybe studies like these have gained so little attention because we already know, vaguely, that smartphones dent concentration – how could a buzzing, flashing computer in our pocket have any other effect? But people tend to treat attention span like some discrete mental faculty, as if it's the same as skill at arithmetic; nice to have but plenty of folks manage fine without.

Researchers at Cambridge University showed recently that eye contact synchronizes the brainwaves of infant and parent which helps with communication and learning. "When the adult and the infant are looking at each other, they are signalling their availability and intention to communicate with each other," said lead researcher Dr Victoria Leong. That doesn't mean breastfeeding mothers need to lock eyes with their children 24 hours a day, but texting mothers may be missing out on vital bonding time with their babies.

While email and mobile technology have greatly accelerated the way we do business, Researcher Leslie Perlow argues that the always 'on' mentality can have a long-term detrimental effect on many organizations. Professor Perlow is the Konsuke Matsushita Professor of Leadership at the Harvard Business School and author of *Sleeping With Your Smartphone*.

In her sociological experiments at Boston Consulting Group and other organizations, Perlow has found that if the team – rather than just individuals – collectively rallies around a goal or personal value, it unleashes a process that creates better work and better lives.

Harvard University research suggests that, in a way, the mere presence of our smartphones is like the sound of our names; they are constantly calling to us, exerting a gravitational pull on our attention. If you have ever felt a 'phantom buzz' you inherently know this. Attempts to block or resist this pull takes a toll by impairing our cognitive abilities. In a poignant twist, then, this means that when we are *successful* at resisting the urge to attend to our smartphones, we may actually be undermining our own cognitive performance.

Are you affected? Most likely. Consider the most recent meeting or lecture you attended: did anyone have their smartphone out on the table? Think about the last time you went to the movies, or went out with friends, read a book, or played a game: was your smartphone close by? In all of these cases, merely having your smartphone present may have impaired your cognitive functioning.

Data also shows that the negative impact of smartphone presence is most pronounced for individuals who rank high on a measure capturing the strength of their connection to their phones –that is, those who strongly agree with statements such as: 'I would have trouble getting through a normal day without my cell phone' and 'it would be painful for me to give up my cell phone for a day'. In a world where people increasingly rely on their phones, it is only logical to expect this effect to become stronger and more universal.

We are clearly not the first to take note of the potential costs of smartphones. Think about the number of fatalities associated with driving while talking on the phone or texting, or of texting while walking. Even hearing your phone ring while you're busy doing something else can boost your anxiety. Knowing we have missed a text message or call leads our minds to wander, which can then impair performance on tasks that require sustained attention and undermine our enjoyment.

Beyond these cognitive and health-related consequences, smartphones may impair our social functioning. Having your smartphone out can distract you during social experiences and make them less enjoyable.

With all these costs in mind, however, we must consider the immense value that smartphones provide. In the course of a day you may use your smartphone to get in touch with friends, family, and co-workers; order products online; check the weather; trade stocks; read the Harvard Business Review; navigate your way to a new address – and more. Evidently smartphones increase our efficiency, allowing us to save time and money, connect with others, become more productive, and remain entertained.

So how do we resolve this tension between the costs and benefits of our smartphones?

Well, smartphones have distinct uses. There are situations in which our smartphones provide a key value, such as when they help us get in touch with someone we're trying to meet, or when we use them to search for information that can help us make better decisions. Those are great moments to have our phones nearby. But, rather than allowing smartphones to take over our lives, we should take back the reins. When our smartphones aren't directly necessary, and when being fully and cognitively available is important, setting aside a period of time to put them away out of touch, sight and hearing can be quite valuable.

With these findings in mind, students, employees, and CEOs alike may wish to maximize their productivity by defining windows of time during which they plan to be separated from their phones, allowing them to accomplish tasks requiring deeper thought. Asking employees not to use their phones during meetings may not be enough.

In the past, I have suggested that having meetings without phones can boost focus, function, and the ability to come up with creative solutions. More broadly, we can all become more engaged and cognitively adept in our everyday lives simply by putting our smartphones (far) away. Leslie Perlow's research demonstrates the gains of scheduling 'predictable time off' (PTO) from our smartphones to increase efficiency and collaboration, heightened job satisfaction, and better work-life balance with our relationships.

CHAPTER SIX

Telecommuting: beneficial – or not so much?

*"Being self-employed means you work 12 hours a day for
yourself so you don't have to work eight hours a day for
someone else."*

Oliver Markus Malloy, *Inside the Mind of an Introvert*

Telecommuting has made the news a lot in recent years.
Technology has enabled this growing trend and more
and more companies were taking advantage of it before 2020
arrived. Since then, of course, working from home has become
the norm.

This has been an unprecedented time during which many
who did not and perhaps never would have had the option to
telecommute had no choice but to learn how to do it. This
experience has elicited an array of reactions and results across the
nation and around the world.

Along with social distancing, working from home – now
widely referred to as 'wfh' in company missives and reports – has
become part of the new normal. In tandem with the isolation
wfh brings, mental health has become a bigger national concern.
During lockdown, of course, we weren't just missing face-to-

face contact with our colleagues, we were also isolated from loved ones and personal support systems.

New studies are popping up everywhere assessing the benefits and the downsides of social distancing and remote working. These studies examine an incredibly wide range of impacts of these new ways of working, from the amplification of individual fears and vulnerabilities, to a rise in the phenomenon of virtual meetings that might be the future of work.

In a very serious pre Covid-19 lesson, I met with a family office that had invested heavily in a small company three years earlier. While discussing the family's portfolio, the issue of this particular company came to the fore; it had been badly led and money and investment was being wasted. The company had developed a remote working operation but had also manipulated the overall code of operations and business ethics beyond recognition. The family office had taken ownership of the small company's operations and it was now being managed remotely.

Although remote working can bring savings, particularly on office space rental, it can also be risky. Consider the implications, for instance, if homeworkers begin to use personal electronic devices for official correspondence; security measures to protect the company's reputation and data are an essential part of handling remote staff.

Security of client information and the firm's servers are also a huge concern. Unlike an office setting, where the IT department can easily control access to information because all the machines are in one building, remote workers are far more difficult to monitor. This brings us to the main reason most employers are not in favour of homeworking: they don't trust their workforce, according to Cary Cooper, Professor of

Organizational Psychology and Health at Lancaster University Management School.

"They'll never say that, but that's what it's about. Managers want people in the office because they want to see their little empires there in front of them," he says. "It's totally about trust, and the incompetence of managers who don't know how to manage people remotely."

Telecommuting is one of the new terms for this new way of working remotely and, on the face of it, seems to be the perfect arrangement for workers in dozens of industries. And for the most part, it is. Companies that encourage and support remote work often report higher levels of employee retention and engagement, reduced turnover, higher employee satisfaction, increased productivity and autonomy, and lots of other benefits.

Back in March 2015 I posted *Is telecommuting to be considered or banned?* on my blog. Its essence was a discussion about Yahoo's decision to ban the option of remote working although the company had, for many years, predicted working from home as the future for everybody.

When a memo from HR dropped into the inbox of Yahoo staff taking the homeworking option away, it prompted anger from many of its recipients, not least because of the reasons given. "Some of the best decisions and insights come from hallway and cafeteria discussions, meeting new people, and impromptu team meetings," the memo said. "Speed and quality are often sacrificed when we work from home." The move to get staff back into the office is thought to have been driven by the then-new chief executive Marissa Mayer who herself had returned to work weeks after giving birth.

She may have had a point. While the fallout from Covid-19

may have driven many employers' decisions to increase remote working and seize on the opportunity to cut down on the amount of office space they need, or channel commuting time into business-productive work, the end of those real opportunities for purposeful face-to-face discussions will have a real effect on every aspect of business, from strategy to execution.

In May 2017, IBM made the decision to call its remote workers back to the office. This was a huge surprise to many, given that IBM has long been a staunch supporter of remote work environments for its employees. The official reason was that the company believed greater productivity happens when teams of workers are physically together 'shoulder to shoulder.' A number of other enterprises then made the same decision, Aetna and Bank of America being just two examples.

Why did IBM pull thousands of its workers back into the workplace? Was it, in fact, the desperate move of a company whose profits had fallen, as some pundits suggest? Or did something else trigger them and companies like Yahoo, Aetna and Best Buy to pull back their working from home policies, and prevent corporations like Apple and Google from even attempting it?

Consider, for instance, the increasing emphasis on collaboration and the corresponding realization that any collaborative effort is highly dependent upon well-developed personal relationships among participants. While remote workers might be highly efficient with individual efforts, nothing builds collaborative relationships better than being physically present.

In face-to-face encounters, our brains process the continual cascade of nonverbal cues that we use as the basis for building trust and professional intimacy. Face-to-face interaction is information-rich.

We interpret what people say to us only partially from the words they use. We get most of the message (and all of the emotional nuance behind the words) from vocal cues, facial expressions, and physical movements. And we rely on non-verbal feedback – the instantaneous responses of others – to help us gauge how well our ideas are being accepted.

So potent is the non-verbal link between individuals that, when we are in genuine rapport with someone, we subconsciously match our body positions, movements, and even our breathing rhythms with theirs. Most interestingly, the brain's 'mirror neurons' mimic not just other people's behaviours, but their feelings as well. (A reaction referred to as 'emotional contagion'.)

But companies are not the only ones dealing with issues of a remote workforce. Those who are self-employed or intermittently employed as part of the new gig economy also face challenges that can hinder their productivity and job satisfaction.

Whether you are managed or working for yourself, you may face some or all of these challenges that negatively impact your work life and productivity:

The feeling of being disconnected. Even though there are great tools now for video chat and conferencing, there is still a disconnect if a remote worker sees their team members physically together at the office while they physically removed.

Interruptions. The ability to focus on the task at hand is critical for remote workers. And yet they often feel a need to respond quickly and immediately to any messages they receive from the 'home' office. These can come via chat or email and so the worker finds themselves constantly either checking to see if messages are coming in or responding to an alert or a message. Each of these interruptions means taking focus away from a task and then attempting to get it back once again.

You never really 'leave' work. When people work in offices, they leave at the end of the day. Sure, they may take some work home with them on occasion, but they physically remove themselves from their workplace. Gig and remote workers do not do this – their workspace is right there, 24 hours a day. This leads to the ongoing temptation to skip that after-dinner walk or kid's sports game in favour of moving back into that office space and trying to get more done.

Loneliness. Working remotely is somewhat a lonely proposition. Some people, particularly introverts, love this arrangement. Others, not so much. And the problem is that continuous isolation can lead to mental health issues and even increased mortality. Only you know whether you can be happy and productive in a remote work environment, and you may have to actually try it out for a period of time before you do have the answer for yourself.

Risk to long-term career growth. As a remote worker, you will not have a lot of visibility within the company. If you are ultimately looking for a C-level position, then your choice to work remotely is the wrong one. You need to be physically present to gain the visibility you need for those major promotions.

Final thought: if relationships are the key to innovation and collaboration, trust is at its heart. When it comes to developing trust, there's no substitution for getting people talking and working face-to-face. Building trust is a multi-sensory process, and it's only when people are physically together that they are able to use all their senses.

At my seminars on collaborative leadership, audience members tell me about the challenges and frustrations of trying to get their virtual teams to bond. Although it can be done, various studies confirm that it is more difficult to build trust in virtual teams, harder for informal leaders to emerge, tougher to create genuine dialogue, and easier for misunderstandings to escalate.

It is a fact that remote workers are part of business reality today. But in our world of video meetings and teleconferences, it is all too easy to overlook the value of face-to-face encounters and the boundaries and norms that office working puts in place.

CHAPTER SEVEN

The importance of purposeful leadership

"When you listen with empathy to another person, you give that person psychological air."

Stephen M.R. Covey

We hear a lot about 'purposeful' and 'purpose-driven' leaders and organizations. But what does that really mean, and does it make a difference?

Talk of purposeful leadership has been prompted by growing levels of distrust and disillusionment around the short-termist financial imperatives that are perceived to drive contemporary firms. Typically, the attributes of purposeful organizations – societal responsibility, values and ethics – can simply be translated into the qualities that should characterize their ideal leaders. But what type of leaders do truly purposeful organizations really need?

My own definition of a purposeful leader is one who has a strong moral self, communicates a clear vision for his or her team and takes an ethical approach to leadership that is marked by a commitment to stakeholders.

What is purpose?

Purpose is an aspirational reason for being that inspires and provides a call to action for an organization, its partners, stakeholders, and society as a whole. Strategic research has consistently shown that purpose enables organizations to perform well in times of volatility. That research joins a growing body of evidence demonstrating that a strong and active purpose raises employee engagement and acts as a unifier. It makes customers more loyal and committed to working with you and helps to frame effective decision-making in an environment of uncertainty. The EY Global Leadership Forecast 2018 found that getting purpose right builds organizational resilience and, crucially, improves long-term financial performance.

Independent research from Linkage found connections between purposeful leaders and business results: the companies they led had 2.5 times higher sales growth, four times higher profit growth, five times higher 'competitive differentiation and innovation' scores, and nine times higher employee engagement scores. Companies that create lasting leadership impact differentially invest in developing purposeful leaders and they take concrete steps to assess the organizational dynamics that shape leadership performance.

What outcomes can purposeful leadership influence, and what are the constraints on injecting purpose into an organization's culture? My extensive research reveals the following:

- Purposeful leadership and its constituent components of purposeful leadership – moral self, commitment to stakeholders and vision – are important in influencing a range of employee outcomes; these include intent to quit, job satisfaction, willingness to go the extra mile, sales performance and lower levels of cynicism. Ethical leadership approaches are also central to employees' experience of their work. Employers should consider ways of creating and embedding a purposeful and ethical approach throughout their organization.

- Vision is especially important, for employees and leaders alike, to provide a sense of direction to guide activities. However, multiple or conflicting visions can emerge over time and in different departments or units, causing a sense of confusion and uncertainty. Organizations should aim for alignment around a set of core themes.

- There is much that organizations can do to foster purposeful and ethical leadership by putting in place appropriate central policies, leader role-modelling, training and development and strong organizational values and culture.

- Constraints that might sabotage efforts to develop a purposeful approach to leadership include pressures on time and resources, unrealistic targets, communication errors – including over-communication – remoteness of the organizational centre, and cultural factors such as risk-aversion. Organizations should be aware of issues such as these.

- Organizations tend to focus on a limited range of stakeholders and discount others from their decision-making. However, this can lead to an imbalance in how the organization relates to its wider setting. To combat this, consider strategies such as creating working groups to evaluate the impact of important decisions on a wide range of stakeholders.

What is leadership?

Let's now move on to leadership itself. My view is that leadership is the ability to motivate groups of people towards a common goal, and this is an incredibly important skill in today's business world. Without strong leadership, many otherwise good businesses fail. Understanding what makes a strong leader and how those skills are cultivated is paramount for those pursuing a career in business.

Many of the world's most respected leaders have several personality traits in common. Among the most recognizable are the ability to initiate change and inspire a shared vision, and knowing how to 'encourage the heart' by modelling the skills and behaviours necessary to achieve the stated objectives. Good leaders must also be confident enough in themselves to enable others to contribute and succeed.

Let's now consider some of the most recognized model leaders from the past and their key attributes.

The ability to initiate change — Franklin D. Roosevelt

Good leaders are never satisfied with the status quo and usually aim to change it. They bring about change for the common good by involving others in the process. FDR sought practical ways to help struggling men and women make a better world for themselves and their children. His philosophy was, "bold, persistent experimentation…Take a method and try it. If it fails, admit it frankly and try another. But above all, try something." Being willing to take risks by trying new ideas and involving others in the process of change is a key quality of strong leaders.

Inspiring a shared vision — Martin Luther King

Leaders, through their words and actions, must have the ability to draw others into a common vision by being clear about where they intend to go and persuading others to join them on the journey. Martin Luther King's vision of a country free from racial segregation and discrimination, so poignantly expressed in his famous "I have a dream…" speech, exemplifies this critical leadership trait. King had a vision of a better America, and his ability to bring both white and black people together to march against segregation changed America profoundly.

Modelling leadership — Mohandas K. Gandhi

Strong leaders not only need to have a vision and the ability to initiate change; they must also model the values, actions, and behaviours necessary to make the vision reality. Gandhi created and promoted philosophies of passive resistance and constructive non-violence, and he also lived by these principles. As Indian Prime Minister Indira Gandhi said, "More than his words, his life was his message." By choosing to consistently live and work in a manner that exemplified the values he believed in, Gandhi engendered trust, becoming a role model for others looking to effect change without resorting to violence.

Encouraging the heart — Sir Winston Churchill

29 December 1940, London was hit by one of the most devastating aerial attacks of World War II. Somehow St. Paul's Cathedral survived. Two days later a photo taken by Herbert

Mason, chief photographer of the Daily Mail, showed the dome of St. Paul's among the ruins, silhouetted against billowing smoke and flames. The caption ran: *It symbolizes the steadiness of London's stand against the enemy: the firmness of right against wrong.* Churchill recognized the importance of St. Paul's for national morale and issued the order, "At all costs, St. Paul's must be saved." Leaders must be able to encourage the hearts of those who share their vision, providing a sense of confident optimism even in the face of enormous difficulties.

What is your purpose?

Purpose goes beyond our physical and emotional needs. Being driven by a purpose or a mission takes us beyond focus on our basic needs and into a mode of action where we set goals that we want to achieve.

When we are driven by purpose, we look for meaning in what we do; ways to create enrichment and happiness in our lives. In that context, purpose means identifying our reason for being.

Today, many of us increasingly look to our professional lives to provide us with meaning. That is why one of the key tasks of effective leaders is to ignite a deeper sense of purpose in their employees.

Purpose ties the organization together.

When an organization delivers excellent service, it is because its employees know what they do and why they do it. They are, therefore, able to bring people together for a common cause that is the backbone of what they do, namely, their purpose. It is the job of an organization and its leaders to give employees this sense of purpose and make it the driving force to achieve the intended outcomes.

Making sure that an organization's purpose and mission are fully aligned is probably one of the most effective ways to engage both consumers and employees. However, we all know that it is hard enough to find individual purposes in life that creates meaning and motivate us. So how can this be done for a whole organization with many diverse people?

How do we lead with purpose?

- *What shared purpose articulates a clear purpose for our organization?* Focus on answering the 'why' questions. Why do we exist? What do our employees and stakeholders care about? What resonates with customers?
- *How can we use purpose as a lens for everything we do?* Let purpose guide the solutions you offer, how you treat your customers, and how you engage your workforce.
- *Communicate success stories to all constituents.* Stories perpetuate purpose. Each time people repeat them, purpose entwines more closely with day-to-day business.
- *Integrate purpose into the company's DNA.* Reinforce purpose through the day-to-day customer and employee experience. Treat purpose as a commitment to stakeholders and publicly update on its progress.
- *Focus on leaders: help them develop their own 'why.'* Work with all leaders to articulate their own purpose as it relates to the overarching purpose for the business. Then help them do the same for their teams and employees.
- *Develop key skills.* Purpose-driven leaders form teams, inspire, and motivate in a fast-changing world. They develop psychological safety and agility.

In my book *Purposeful Discussions,* I take purpose across everything we do in organizations, covering emotional intelligence, human-to-human interaction, human relationships, strategy, government, geopolitics, compliance, regulation and even cybercrime. I offer conclusions on life growth, lifelong learnings, personal development and mentorship, and I conclude with the takeaways that we should all arm ourselves with to survive the next decade, to co-create a more sustainable future.

My overall conclusion on purposeful business leadership in today's disruptive world is a balanced view of universal characteristics and traits which has the potential to guide us through years of transformation with optimism and idealism. To conclude, the first step towards inspiring others, and thus beginning the personal transition from managing to leading, is to understand your own purpose. If you aspire to become a leader, you also need to find an organization that will accommodate your purpose because it is only when we set sail on the right course with smart individuals that our purposeful journey, progress and performance become so much more worthwhile.

CHAPTER EIGHT

Purpose is more than 'correct' policy and practice

*"Technology is not an exogenous force over which we
have no control. We are not constrained by a binary choice
between 'accept and live with it' and 'reject and live
without it'. Instead, take dramatic technological change as
an invitation to reflect about who we are and how we see
the world. The more we think about how to harness the
technology revolution, the more we will examine ourselves
and the underlying social models that these technologies
embody and enable, and the more we will have an
opportunity to shape the revolution in a manner that
improves the state of the world."*

Klaus Schwab, engineer and founder of the World
Economic Forum

Business today is subject to the rapid exhaustion of constant change, and constant change seems to be pushing leadership to its limits. Windows of opportunity are shorter and companies are forced out of business quicker.

If we revisit the 1950s, the average life of a company was just over 60 years. Today it is less than 20 years. The reason for this decline in company life longevity, according to a recent study by Credit Suisse, is disruptive technology, yet disruptive technologies are not new. The credit card, the microwave oven, transistor radio, television, computer hard disks, solar cells, optic fibre, plastic and the microchip were all introduced in the 1950s.

It is not technology that explains failure despite costly investments; it is more about leaders' failure to envision the future of their business as the world changes around them. It is the result of short-sightedness, an inability to anticipate the future and then adapt and lead with a focused, flexible strategy in a changing world.

For humans to be effective, productive and innovative, we must have great leaders who also focus on injecting into organizational life the qualities of trust, humility, accountability, experimentation, collaboration, digitization and innovation within a commercially astute context. Doing this ensures that their people and their company constantly deliver increased value for customers. It also ensures that they drive success within their ever-expanding areas of influence and responsibility so that the business flows and flourishes in uncertain times.

The purpose of a company is not just to make money but to pursue a just cause. We should all remind ourselves of the words of Henry Ford: "A business that makes nothing but money is a poor kind of business."

Purpose is the very reason to have the business. It's not marketing. It's not a recruiting tool. It's not something you just write on your website. It's not a corporate social responsibility programme. It is, instead, the very reason why you started the business in the first place, and it has nothing to do with money.

To be truly purpose-driven, the most senior leader will still see themselves as subservient to a higher purpose, answering not to another organization's human being but to an ideal. We are in service of those ideals and although we will never actually achieve them, we will die trying and that is the point: it's about progress, not just prosperity. Prosperity is counting what comes in; progress is counting how far we've moved down a purposeful path. The people who work at truly purpose-driven organizations feel like they belong, that this is their calling. It has nothing to do with the business or the product.

Companies exist to advance and innovate, push technology on or improve quality of life, looking for ways to harness potential and ease or enhance our lives in some way, shape or form. That people are willing to pay money for whatever a company has to offer is the proof that they perceive or derive some value from those things, which means the more value a company offers, the more money and the more advancement the company will have for further progression.

Capitalism has to be more about prosperity, about progress.

We have all seen the increase in certain practices that drive stock price value up in the short term and all these deals certainly sound ethically dubious. The importance of business ethics reaches far beyond employee loyalty and morale or the strength of a management team bond. As with all business initiatives, the ethical operation of a company is directly related to profitability in both the short and long term. A business' reputation in its surrounding community with other businesses and individual investors, is paramount in determining whether a company is a worthwhile investment. If a company is perceived to operate unethically, investors are less inclined to buy stock or otherwise support its operations.

Technology companies like Facebook, Twitter and Google

certainly look like they are more comfortable asking for forgiveness for ethical misconduct than leading the charge with a proactive view of how they might safeguard one of their most important assets – our private data. You could question how these companies can operate without transparent accountability.

The responsibility of business is to use its will and resources to advance a cause greater than itself, protect the people and places in which it operates and generate more resources so that it can continue doing all those things for as long as possible. An organization can do whatever it likes to build its business so long as it accepts responsibility for the consequences of its actions.

Leadership is the lifeblood of an organization. When leaders create safe environments at work, everyone thrives and devotion is the natural response to those conditions. Toxic cultures breed cynicism, paranoia, and self-interest. The responsibility of a company is to serve the customer. The responsibility of leadership is to serve their people so that their people may better serve the customer. If leaders fail to serve their people first, customer and company will suffer.

The management team sets the tone for how the entire company runs on a day-to-day basis. When the prevailing management philosophy is based on ethical practices and behaviour, leaders within an organization can direct employees by example and guide them in making decisions that are not only beneficial to them as individuals, but also to the organization as a whole. Building on a foundation of ethical behaviour helps create long-lasting purposeful effects for a company, for instance, the ability to attract and retain highly talented individuals or building and maintaining a purposeful reputation within the community. Running a business in an ethical manner from the top down builds a stronger bond between individuals on the management team, further creating stability within the company.

Globally, successful entrepreneurs are emerging as exciting, courageous and authentic new role models who demonstrate many of the vital qualities required for effective 21st-century leadership in the future of work. They are reinventing how to apply entrepreneurship and intrapreneurship practices to harness potential and mobilize human energy towards creating a better future.

This suggests that 21st-century leadership learning programmes are most effective when they focus on cultivating new mindsets alongside creative, critical and forward-thinking strategies. That develops the ability to anticipate, adapt and cultivate new behaviours and take intelligent actions.

CHAPTER NINE

When the only answer is to make better decisions

*"The leader can never close the gap between himself and
the group. If he does, he is no longer what he must be. He
must walk a tightrope between the consent he must win
and the control he must exert."*

Vince Lombardi, NFL player, coach and executive
director

Recently I had a very early morning meeting with one of my mentors in which we discussed the changes in leadership wrought by the Fourth Industrial Revolution and why leadership needs to understand the emotional wake created by transformation and know when it is time to step down.

Leadership is about defining what the future should look like and getting the board of directors and stakeholders to not only share, but also develop that future together. Being trustworthy and selfless; truthful and compassionate – these are wonderful qualities. If leaders consistently displayed these traits, workplaces and employees would be doing much better. But not all leaders, including many of the most famous and successful, exhibit these qualities.

Leadership is getting smarter about work and people, and the intersection between them. More and more often, working people are telling the truth about topics they were once afraid to talk about openly. One of the stickiest topics is the quality of leadership found in both large and small employers. We are starting to tell the truth about the fact that most people in leadership positions are lacking in critical skills.

At best, many lack listening skills; at worst, they are abusive bullies. Significant data on workplace bullying reports that verbal abuse, shouting, public berating, and the creation of a climate of intimidation is widespread. Research by psychologists from the University of California, Berkeley, has found that when leaders start to feel powerful, many allow more benevolent qualities like empathy to decline. Other studies show that people in positions of corporate power are three times more likely than lower-level employees to interrupt co-workers, multitask during meetings, raise their voices, and say insulting things. They don't know how to talk to their employees and they don't know how to listen. If today's leaders received any management training at all, they were probably trained only to dole out work assignments and evaluate people. They don't know how to probe for understanding or how to create cohesion in a team.

Organizations have always needed leaders who are good at recognizing emerging challenges and inspiring organizational responses. That need is intensifying today as leaders confront, among other things, digitization, the surging power of data as a competitive weapon, and the ability of artificial intelligence to automate the workplace and enhance business performance. These technology-driven shifts create an imperative for most organizations to change and this, in turn, demands more and better leaders up and down the line.

Unfortunately, there is overwhelming evidence that the plethora of services, books, articles, seminars, conferences, and TED-like talks purporting to have the answers are delivering disappointing results. And this is a global industry estimated to be worth more than $50 billion.

According to a recent Fortune survey, only 7 per cent of CEOs believe their companies are building effective global leaders, and just 10 per cent said that their leadership development initiatives have a clear business impact. McKinsey's latest research has a similar message: only 11 per cent of more than 500 executives polled around the globe strongly agreed with the statement that their leadership development interventions achieve and sustain the desired results.

The Fourth Industrial Revolution holds the promise of a new era of globalization in which advanced technologies can drive new opportunities, diverse ideas can be heard, and new forms of communication may come to the fore. However, many senior executives remain less prepared for this great shift than they think they are. A year ago, Deloitte's inaugural survey on private and public sector readiness for the Fourth Industrial Revolution observed a 'tension between hope and ambiguity'. It found that while executives conceptually understood the profound business and societal changes the Fourth Industrial Revolution may bring, they were less certain how they could take action to benefit.

Executives are struggling to develop effective strategies in today's rapidly changing markets. Faced with an ever increasing array of new technologies, leaders acknowledge they have too many options and in some cases lack the strategic vision to help them choose.

Organizational influences also challenge leaders as they seek to navigate this new Industrial Revolution. Many leaders have reported their companies don't follow clearly defined decision-making processes, and organizational silos limit their ability to develop and share knowledge to determine effective strategies. Leaders continue to focus more on using advanced technologies to protect their positions rather than as bold investments to drive disruption. Although many of the businesses that have made investments in technology are seeing payoffs, others are finding it difficult to invest even though digital technologies are creating more global connections and new opportunities within new markets and localized economies. Challenges include being too focused on short-term results and lacking understanding, the ability to make a sound business case, and leadership vision.

Leaders acknowledge the ethical implications inherent in new technology, but few companies are talking about how to manage those challenges, let alone actively putting policies in place to do so. As the skills challenge becomes clearer, so too do differences between executives and their millennial workforces. In 2019 most leaders (86 per cent) thought their organizations were doing enough to create a workforce for the Fourth Industrial Revolution. In 2020, as more leaders recognized the growing skills gap, only 47 per cent were confident in their efforts.

On the bright side, twice as many leaders indicate their organizations will do what they can to train their existing employees rather than hire new ones. And they're more optimistic than they were that autonomous tech will augment, rather than replace, humans.

So how does a leader know when it's time to battle on and when it's time to step aside? If we listen to the internal monologue of today's leader, the discussion goes something like this:

The journey to get where you are has not been easy. From setting records to surviving recessions, you've been there from day one, becoming a leader who is respected and praised by board, shareholders and staff. But somewhere along the way, it all started to change. Now your leadership strategy is getting you nowhere, and you can no longer deny that nagging feeling that something's just not right.

Recognizing that you may not be the best person for the job anymore is incredibly difficult to admit, especially after all the blood, sweat, and tears you've invested in the company. But if that little voice in the back of your head is now shouting at you front and centre, it's likely that others are thinking the same thing. Hanging on too long will make you irrelevant.

Organizations change. Leaders should change too. You may not be the best person to lead your business forward. The skills that worked yesterday may not work today or tomorrow. The bottom line is that successful leaders know when to move on. Are your strengths the right strengths to lead the organization tomorrow?

The most important question a leader should ask themselves is: are you placing the good of the organization first? This is what leadership is all about.

Final thought: most CEOs have become zealous about the impact of accelerating disruption and the need to adapt in response. Time and again, though, we see those same CEOs forgetting about the need to translate strategy into specific organizational capabilities. They pay lip service to their talent ambitions and delegate responsibility to the Head of Learning with a flourish of fine words, only for that individual to complain later about lack of support from above.

To be fair, CEOs are pulled in many directions and they note that leadership development often doesn't make an impact on performance in the short run. At the same time, we see many heads of learning confronting CEOs with a set of complex interwoven interventions and not always focusing on what matters most. But as the pace of change for strategies and business models increases, so does the cost of lagging leadership development.

If CEOs and their top teams are serious about long-term performance, they need to commit themselves to the success of corporate leadership development efforts now. That demands focus on what really matters from C-level human resource executives and heads of learning to simplify their programmes.

PART 2

Strategy

Strategy is about making trust a part of the plan.
This section looks at the key elements of successful and sustainable strategies that grow leaders and build companies. These are factors beyond process and systems. They include the sound ethics that should underpin a health company culture; the vital role played by clear communication of trust, purpose and context; the need to put respect front and foremost in client relationships; and the authentic leadership that earns legitimacy.

Build strategy on these pillars and reap the engagement dividend.

CHAPTER TEN

Leaders need legitimacy

"To be trusted is a greater compliment than to be loved."
George MacDonald

I recently reread Malcolm Gladwell's latest book, *David and Goliath.* Like his previous works, I enjoyed it a great deal. I see Gladwell as kind of a social facilitator and observer. He doesn't try to present himself as a behavioural scientist with countless reams of data to support his conclusions; he makes comments and observations, and the reader can choose to accept or reject them.

Given the outcome and the divides exposed during and after the 2016 U.S. Presidential election cycle, I found some of his insights particularly worth revisiting. I enjoyed the entire book, but the part that most spoke to me was Gladwell's discussion of legitimacy.

Legitimacy, Gladwell says, demands three elements:

- The governed have a voice; their input is sought and heard

- There is predictability and consistency in the application of laws or standards
- Laws or standards must be administered fairly and objectively; any disparate treatment must have a clear and compelling reason behind it

From what I have seen, the President elected in 2016 didn't share Gladwell's description of legitimacy. Specifically, his interest in viewpoints that don't coincide with his own appear non-existent and his application of laws and standards have not, in my opinion, passed the fair and objective test.

I personally believe that any meaningful change in our leadership philosophy and application will have to come from the private sector. The Trump administration was interested in a rigid application of the compliance model; that people should do as instructed. The President himself had never been in an environment where he was accountable to anyone, and he seemed to struggle with that transition.

I find this discussion about legitimacy so interesting because of its application to the work environment.

For the last four decades I have been promoting and teaching the merits of an employment relationship based on commitment rather than compliance. When the employment environment is optimized in a commitment-based model it delivers employee engagement.

I also believe that, to a large extent, leadership – as opposed to management – is founded in legitimacy. Leadership is entirely relational and is not hierarchical. As a manager, however, you rely on the authority of your position and the benefit of what Stephen M.R. Covey calls deterrence, the authority that comes from rules or position. We would all like to believe that management also incorporates competence, the second of Covey's three levels of trust, but I am not sure that is true. In many cases the competence we rely on when elevating someone to a management role is based on their technical skills; competence in emotional and social intelligence are still considered 'soft skills' and not essential.

The highest level of trust in Covey's hierarchy is identity-based trust. It incorporates both your competency and your character, as demonstrated by your applied values and behaviour, to create credibility.

In more than forty years as a human resource professional, C-level executive and management consultant, I have found it interesting to see emerging and current 'leaders' bridle at the idea that they must earn trust. Many have the expectation that trust will be embedded in their role and they should not have to earn it.

Any student of the relationship between employer and the employed realizes that up until the 1940s, the concept that employers might need to win legitimacy through the input of their employees was considered ludicrous. Unions fought extremely hard to legitimize their right to bargain with employers over hours, wages, and working conditions. I do not say that collective bargaining is the preferred methodology for building the relationship structure between organizations and employees, but it's certain the concept of participating as equals didn't come from management enlightenment.

It is very chic today to dismiss collective bargaining and unions as passé, and many of our current models still have their roots in the principles of Taylor's Scientific Management: managers manage and workers do. But if you only see people as 'human capital', what is the likelihood that you are seeking the endorsement of those you 'lead'? Surveys come out every year that reinforce the view that the most significant role of human resources professionals is to ensure compliance. Under the old social contract, organizations provided a degree of social and economic security in return for loyalty (in my opinion, another word for compliance). As the economy became more international, we still wanted the loyalty, but we just didn't want to provide the security. It is interesting that in most jurisdictions outside of the U.S., among the topics included in collective bargaining is the introduction of technology into a work setting. In our U.S. model, we must negotiate the effects of the technology but not its introduction.

To create my own foundation for employee engagement, I insist on a number of critical elements. The first is a foundation of trust. I would go as far as to say you have to have trust at all three of Covey's levels – deterrence, competence and identity – to experience true engagement. You then need to add the elements of respect, responsibility, information, equitable rewards, and mutual investment.

I do not think you need to negotiate your culture with employees, but I do think they are entitled to clear expectations, constructive feedback, and fair treatment. When you provide that kind of context you are allowing employees to join up with you. On that foundation, when change is introduced you do it with, rather than to, your people.

Gladwell's examples of authority without legitimacy are fascinating but the outcomes aren't pretty.

We see examples even today in various places across the globe whereby power of military capability or financial resources the view of the few or the many are imposed upon minority populations or neighbors.

A very current example is occurring as we write this in Ukraine, with Russia's decision to invade to "protect" ethnic Russians and create a "barrier" to Western intrusion into some hypothetical safety zone. We saw similar action in Myanmar with the junta asserting control.

Up until the late 1930's in the United States corporate organizations by right of wealth freely imposed their will on workers with the government's implicit and explicit support. Until the Wagner Act, (also known as the National Labor Relations Act) it was perfectly legal for employers to terminate employees attempting to form unions to collectively bargain subjects like wages, hours and working conditions.

It was only in 1964 that discriminating against employees based on color, race, religion, national origin, and other factors were deemed illegal and even later for discrimination based on age.

In 1993 the rights of working parents were finally codified providing protection for childbirth, adoption, and related factors that tended to significantly disadvantage women in the workplace.

He discusses the rising generations now entering the workplace and their intolerance of assumed legitimacy. They will expect to be treated as stakeholders and they are willing to withdraw from employers if they feel that mutual respect and transparency are not fundamental to the business culture presented to them.

The events of the pandemic have underscored this sense of "stakeholdership" as illustrated by the Great Resignation and push back from employees who have worked remotely for almost two years refusing to return to the traditional office setting to satisfy the sense of control that some employers still embrace.

One of the few positive side effects of the recent pandemic is a clear demonstration that how and where work is performed can no longer be taken for granted and some outcomes show positive impacts on productivity and performance rather than the expected decreases.

CHAPTER ELEVEN

Engaged employees need context

"Few things help an individual more than to place responsibility upon him, and to let him know that you trust him."

Booker T. Washington

These days we hear an enormous amount about the concept of employee engagement. I want to be clear about what engagement is and is not, from my perspective.

Engagement is not about happiness, morale, or even necessarily an individual employee's self-actualization. Nor is it a programme. It is about creating alignment between organizational and individual goals and performance and a clear line of sight towards both.

In the mid-1990s I felt like our relationships at work were very flawed and there was a lot of room for improvement. I was lucky to spend the early part of my career as a young human resource professional in an organization that, by the standards of the time, was progressive. I further benefited from being exposed to excellent training and some of the newest concepts in what we today call human resources management.

The organization was an early adopter in our manufacturing facilities of initiatives such as quality circles and we were among the first to look at the increasing costs of health care and to experiment with more long-term alternatives rather than simply changing insurers and increasing the employee's share of the cost. We began exploring and implementing solutions that addressed root causes and the prevention of poor health outcomes. We had conversations with employees about these approaches and how they could help make a difference.

In the early 1980s I had the chance to work in a technologically and geographically isolated division where we were one of two pilot organizations given permission to experiment using a Scanlon Plan, an incentive scheme that moved beyond the traditional piece-rate approach to productivity.

In its most simplistic form, a Scanlon Plan tracks the costs of manufacturing and distributing a product over time and then interjects an employee suggestion process to identify and make improvements. If the 'plan' yields savings, a portion of those savings are shared with employees, typically as a monthly or quarterly bonus. For me, the most important part of this model was not the bonus but that the programme was led by a cross-functional and multi-level committee that reviewed each employee suggestion in a monthly meeting to determine which would be moved forward.

This seemed to me to be a significant step forward from the traditional Quality Circle because of the breadth and depth of the steering committee, and the way in which the approach directly tied an opportunity to affect a workers' compensation to the system.

While the initiative wasn't an unqualified success, we did see a much higher degree of collaboration; we were able to introduce into the equation the management of the costs of providing health care and our losses from work-related injuries because people saw themselves as active participants in the process and the outcomes. I know this isn't rocket science, but it clearly demonstrated that people will bring more to their work if they see a compelling reason why they should and are offered a benefit beyond a simple financial reward.

This was the early 1980s and no one had yet labelled this kind of model, but I was fascinated. So began my journey of looking around for other new models that could shift perspectives and practice. Twenty years later, on a dusty shelf at a client's office, I discovered a book that affected me profoundly.

In his 1991 book *Why This Horse Won't Drink,* Ken Matejka describes commitment:

"Commitment is the act of being physically, psychologically, and emotionally impelled. It means that employees gladly give up other options."

In this model, employees choose you and your organization over any of their other available choices; you have become partners in your organizational mission! This creates a powerful image. If you are a CEO or a business owner, it almost sounds like a fantasy. I would submit to you that creating and sustaining this kind of commitment can indeed be done, but to see it become reality you must commit as a leader to a systemic approach and follow through.

Roger Deprey created a well-known HR model, the Human Resources Pyramid, a series of six questions that he believed every employee asks in a particular order:

- What is my job?
- How am I doing?

- Does anyone really care?
- What is our function/mission/goal?
- How are we doing?
- How can I help?

Deprey further stated that in less than 15 per cent of organizations around the world do their employees reach the final question: how can I help? I studied this model thirty years ago and my experience since has convinced me that Deprey was right.

A 2004 study by the Hudson Institute supports that concern; they reported that in a national multiple-industry survey with several thousand respondents, less than half of employees felt 'loyal' to their employer, and a third said they did not expect to be with their current employer longer than another 18 to 24 months. These proportions were higher in certain industries such as transportation, communications, public administration, and government, where dissatisfaction numbers were over 60 per cent. The study also identified a direct correlation between 'loyalty' and productivity.

The numbers since that 2004 study have become progressively worse. At this point, we have some of the lowest engagement scores since we began tracking employee morale and satisfaction. Not only does this cost us trillions annually in productivity 'bleed', we now know unequivocally that poor engagement also has financial impact, including the health care costs of work-related accidents and injuries, depression and stress. You could point out that 2004 was a long time ago, and you would be right, but I would say that the recession of 2008 and the effects of the current pandemic tell us we have not made significant strides since then.

When I built my original model, *Moving from Compliance to Commitment*™, I incorporated Deprey's six questions firmly into the foundation of my work.

Think about your own organization and whether your employees have the answers to the first five questions, and whether they are asking themselves or their manager the last question. If you can say yes, congratulations – you have a committed or engaged workforce and a management team positioned for change and success. If not, you may want to continue reading.

Corporations and organizations spend an enormous amount of time and money talking to employees, shareholders and other stakeholders about mission, vision, culture, and values as abstract principles. Before employees can embrace your vision or mission, they need to understand where they personally fit in the organization and how you, as an executive, see them and their contributions.

That may not be very sexy, but it is the reality.

To me, these things represent the foundation of what we have begun over the last decade or so to describe as employee engagement. I think so many of those engagement initiatives continue to fail because they are approached as a programme rather than a fundamental shift in culture.

Another reality: the vision and mission must be embraced at the frontline (customer-facing) level which requires frontline supervisors to both embrace and reinforce values through actions. Remember that employees live with supervisor expectations and conflicting priorities every day. They see the reality of actions contrasted with the abstractions of vision and mission statements.

For the typical employee, we are much weaker at answering

Deprey's first three questions: what is my job? How am I doing? Does anyone care?

I have seen system after system that describes an organization's values and culture while that same system reinforces a different set of values through its actions in hiring, promotion, performance management and other related operations. Clarity, and through clarity engagement starts with modelling the values you espouse to your employees.

I support Deprey's key point that for employees to sign up and support the corporate vision, you must answer those first three questions. Just as starving people do not focus on self-actualization, employees who do not understand the basic context of their job and how it contributes to the big picture will not focus on the corporate mission or achieve their personal best.

Typically, leaders get the results for which they manage; if you manage for excellence, you get it. If on the other hand you manage for 'good', you get average. The critical path here is the behaviour for which you manage at the frontline level. How many times do you see an organization where the average level of performance is assessed as 3.5 or 4 out of 5, yet it fails to meet its organizational goals?

Although it is not the role of C-level executives to have daily conversations with frontline employees about where they fit into the big picture, it is their role to ensure that the systems and culture are in place to reinforce the values and behaviours they want to see in their company.

Do your frontline managers have the required people skills and understand their critical role in this process? Are they being hired, trained, and rewarded for these skill sets? Or are they being hired solely for their 'technical' skills?

CHAPTER TWELVE

The employee engagement dividend

*"When the pace of change outside an organization becomes
greater than the pace of change inside the organization, the
end is near."*

John R. Walter, President, ATT

Starting out in the early 1980s as a young human resource
professional, I began to recognize that there were significant
flaws in the way that we managed the relationship between
employer and employed.

I had entered the mining industry full of self-righteous
indignation about the fact that, in this age of enlightenment, an
anachronism like unions and collective bargaining continued
to exist. I felt very clearly that the collective bargaining process
was totally unnecessary. Employers had grown to appreciate the
importance of the employed and it was no longer necessary to
have third party intervention.

As you read this you are smiling at my youthful arrogance and
naiveté. That began the journey that I charted in my first book,
Managing Whole People. I won't bore you with the full premise I
set out there, other than to say that I had not yet seen the concept

of employee engagement widely proliferated. In fact, in the absence of that concept, I created my own model and described it as moving from compliance to commitment, or C2C.

I was very lucky in my early corporate career to have had the opportunity to participate in new models such as Total Quality, self-directed work teams and several other initiatives that at the time were considered very *avant garde*. However, I still felt there was something missing and so I kept refining my own model. As part of my subsequent journey, I immersed myself in the work of thinkers such as BlessingWhite Consulting, Rhoads and Whitlark, Patrick Lencioni and Malcolm Gladwell, among others.

I also started to see more discussion on what is now commonly referred to as employee engagement. I was very excited to discover there was a name for what I was trying to accomplish and, more importantly, that scientific research was beginning to emerge that quantified its effects. What happened when a large portion of the workforce was unengaged?

Eric Allenbaugh, a Lake Oswego-based managed consultant, published an article describing the three primary cultures represented in corporate America:

- The 'glazed-eye group', most recognizable through their lack of spirit and vitality. They are adept at explaining why something can't be done; they make excuses and avoid taking risks or being accountable at all costs. Here is the really bad news – Allenbaugh estimates this population is 54 per cent of the American workforce and, since their attitude ranges from neutral to mildly negative, they don't take proactive action to improve their situation.

Let me be specific here: what I mean is they don't leave under their own power; they stay and drain the energy out of your organization.

- The 'beady-eyed group' is actively disengaged. They are your corporate terrorists. They actively seek out the flaws and the negatives and 'spread the wealth', sharing their negative energy and disenchantment with everybody. Although they represent only about 17 per cent of the workforce their impact is disproportionate: they consume huge amounts of managerial energy and investment; they are not interested in finding solutions and improving things; they are also not significantly more likely than the glazed-eye group to seek alternative employment either. Since 'life sucks', they figure it's all the same everywhere, so why go to the effort of changing?

- The 'bright-eyed group' is the group you want, period. These folks are engaged, they buy into your mission, values, and vision. They embrace change, look for opportunities to improve their skills and aptitudes and embrace personal accountability. The unfortunate part is that they represent only about 29 per cent of the current workforce.

Before I talk about solutions, I want to share a little more perspective with you to create the sense of urgency we need to tackle the cost of 'presenteeism'.

A study by Cigna Healthcare provides some startling statistics and illustrates what HR professionals mean when they talk about presenteeism:

- U.S. workers reported that they spend two to five hours per week resolving personal issues at work, at a productivity loss of 5–12 per cent.
- 61 per cent of U.S. workers have reported to work while they were ill or dealing with personal matters.
- Of that group, 62 per cent felt that they were noticeably less productive or attentive to their duties at these times.
- 46 per cent had missed at least one day of work in the preceding six months, with 22 per cent of those absences related to family matters.

A National Mental Health Association study has estimated that the costs of productivity lost to presenteeism are over $200 billion annually. Let's put that in perspective: that means in three and a half years we reach the point where these losses are equal to the Federal bailout! These losses were calculated before we entered our current financial crisis, and I would venture to suggest that the scores have not improved since then.

So now, hopefully, I have your attention. Let's talk about some of the solutions that might address these issues. I talk about them in much more detail in *Managing Whole People*, but I'll give you an overview here.

Hire hard, manage easy. My friend and colleague Joseph Skursky of Market Leader Solutions, uses this motto as the basis of his recruitment and selection system. I describe it briefly in *Hire Right!* The point is to be careful about who you let in your lifeboat! Starting with the right folks makes it a whole lot easier, trust me!

Create an appropriate culture. I have spent the last fifteen years refining my *Moving from Compliance to*

Commitment™ model. It is composed of five elements: respect, responsibility, information, rewards, and loyalty. My premise is simple – people join and stay with cultures, not organizations. As leaders you are the guardian of the culture. You notice I say 'join up'. They make an affirmative choice to join up or commit to you. In *Why This Horse won't Drink*, Ken Matejka describes commitment like this: "Commitment is the act of being physically, psychologically, and emotionally impelled. It means that employees gladly give up other options." Now think of those glazed and beady-eyed folks I described and tell me that physically, psychologically, and emotionally impelled doesn't sound better!

Good Leadership. Good leadership is critical, but what is it? I like Marcus Buckingham's definition:

> *"Effective leaders don't have to be passionate. They don't have to be charming. They don't have to be brilliant...*
> *They don't have to be great speakers. What they must be is clear. Above all else, they must never forget the truth that of all the human universals...our need for clarity is the most likely to engender in us confidence, persistence, resilience, and creativity."*

> The One Thing You Need to Know ... (2005)

What do you think about that?

Clarity. Who are we? What are we trying to accomplish? What is my role? Every employee asks these questions. Our job is to answer them.

Effective management. Management is different from leadership, period. Richard Rumelt, a professor of Management at UCLA describes the role of management this way:

"The most important role of any manager is to break down a situation into challenges a subordinate can handle. The manager absorbs a great chunk of the ambiguity in the situation and gives much less ambiguous problems to others."

When you combine these elements, you have created a 'culture of engagement'. I am not going to tell you that you ever 'arrive', but you will perform at a place where you want to be.

Recent thinking from Pepper and Rogers and BlessingWhite Consulting show us some impressive reasons why engagement is important and what kind of outcomes you might expect.

One is a new view of engagement which distinguishes between the traditional view of the intellectual, behavioural, and emotional elements we have traditionally associated with engagement. To describe those a little more fully, the intellectual level is where an employee agrees with your company vision statement and/or a customer values the attributes of your brand. The behavioural level – recommending or purchasing your product or service – is where you start to see energy or discretionary effort. The third level, the emotional level, is where you see buy-in and enthusiasm. In some ways this parallels Ron Willingham's *Three Dimensions of Congruency*™; the 'I think, I feel, I am'. Willingham pointed out, and Pepper and Rogers agree, that the emotional buy-in is much more impactful than the intellectual appeal.

They go on, however, to describe a different and more comprehensive model which includes five levels and incorporates critical concepts like satisfaction, quality, and loyalty. These 'new' levels in hierarchical order are: satisfied, loyal, recommend, best products and services, and pride. Most importantly, they also describe the critical foundation that this system is based upon, a foundation called trust. The point here, as I have discussed thoroughly, is that without a trust-based relationship the rest of the engagement initiative is a wasted effort – and trust is built at the frontline level between the immediate supervisor and the employee. It is the trust factor that the five elements of *Compliance to Commitment*™ address: respect, responsibility, information, rewards, and loyalty. There is also a clear relationship to the *Human Resources Pyramid*™ described earlier.

The Peppers and Rogers model considers both employee and customer engagement and argues they are inextricably linked. They also say that true engagement affects three critical elements that every organization should be concerned about: productivity, performance, and sustainability.

Importantly, this article provides some definitive numbers in each of the following categories:

Productivity
Depending upon what business you are in, your 'human capital' costs on average represent 60 to 70 per cent of total expenditure. As we know, in some businesses it is much higher. As we point out, the best companies are recognizing this and leveraging their return on investment in this area. A 2008 study by Development Dimensions International (an international training and consulting firm) indicates that moving an employee's level of engagement from low to high returned a 21 per cent increase in individual performance. According to studies by the Society for Human Resources Management and the Hay Group, employees at the highest levels of performance have per capita productivity that is 20 per cent higher than the average across industries, and offices with high levels of engagement are 43 per cent more

productive. Engaged customers also enhance your productivity through repeat business and word of mouth recommendations.

Performance

Engagement also has direct correlation with financial performance. Engaged employees tend to stay with their current employers at a rate of 85 per cent versus 27 per cent for the disengaged, according to international consulting firm BlessingWhite Consulting. The savings from reduced turnover alone are huge.

It doesn't stop with the benefits of employee retention. Highly engaged organizations saw a shareholder return of 24% versus 9.1% year to year from organization with moderate or low engagement.

Similarly retail stores with high engagement outperformed other stores by 36% in operating income over the same period.

Customer engagement shows similar results, including higher loyalty, increased revenue, increased profit and increased wallet share. When you combine high employee and high customer engagement, there is a 100 per cent difference in financial performance on a peer-to-peer basis.

I don't know about you, but those kinds of bottom-line impacts get my attention!

Sustainability

On organizational sustainability, I want to talk about three different areas that Peppers and Rogers identified:

Brand: A 2003 study showed that the experience a customer has with your employees influences repeat purchase decisions so much, that 'they are your brand.' In the same study it was reported that 51 per cent of consumers say 'outstanding service' is the number one reason they continue to do business with an organization and, conversely, 80 per cent will discontinue doing business because of a bad experience.

Strategy: The biggest reason CEOs fail is not bad strategy, but bad implementation of their strategy, according to a study by Ram Charan reported in Fortune magazine. Engaged employees play a critical role in that implementation.

Human capital: Over the next 10 to 15 years the demand for experienced talent is expected to increase by 25 per cent while the supply decreases by 15 per cent. Under these circumstances, retention of critical talent becomes even more important. Remember that engaged employees are 87 per cent less likely to seek alternative employment.

The 2008 BlessingWhite Consulting study referenced earlier says fewer than 30 per cent of employees are engaged. The same study says 19 per cent are 'disengaged'. But it gets worse: disengaged workers are not the most likely to leave – they 'quit and stay'.

The same study found that only 27 per cent of organizations globally have a formal programme or strategy to increase employee engagement and 19 per cent don't even have it on their radar.

This sounds remarkably like the numbers from Allenbaugh doesn't it? Now the punch line: Allenbaugh did his research in 1994, 14 years earlier than BlessingWhite and Pepper and Rogers – look at the productivity we squandered in that period!

So, let's go back to the beginning. In line with our thinking at New Paradigms, the foundation of employee engagement is the same as any healthy relationship – mutual trust between the parties. We believe there is a direct relationship between the five elements of *Compliance to Commitment*™ and building that foundation of trust.

Look at the numbers: $200 billion per year lost to presenteeism, a potential 21 per cent per capita increase in productivity, and significant increases in financial performance and every other key metric. Or we can keep doing what we are doing now.

This Margaret Wheatley quote summarizes it beautifully:

> *"In organizations, real power and energy is generated through relationships. The patterns of relationships and the capacity to form them are more important than tasks, functions, roles, and positions."*
> Leadership and the New Science (1992)

CHAPTER THIRTEEN

Why ethical leadership and conduct matter

"To me, it really seems visible today that ethics is not something exterior to the economy, which, as technical matter, could function on its own; rather, ethics is an interior principle of the economy itself, which cannot function if it does not take account of the human values of solidarity and reciprocal responsibility."

Pope Benedict XVI

In discussion over a coffee with a leader in technology innovation, I wanted to pin down why doing the right thing morally and ethically in leadership can be the right thing to do.

During the pandemic, many tech companies asked employees to stay at home. And also to work, of course. We were discussing the decision of Microsoft CEO, Satya Nadella, in an act of compassion and goodwill, to continue to pay employees their full regular pay.

Have you ever noticed how decisions are so much harder when you try to do the right thing and make an ethical decision, rather than focusing on what's easiest or most practical? This is mainly because the right thing means different things to different people.

The world of business is full of ethical dilemmas, from where to direct scarce resources, through to how a company serves its local community. Every leader will make ethical decisions, whether or not they acknowledge them as such at the time, but whether leadership is based on an ethical framework is determined by *all* the decisions they make.

It's increasingly important to make ethical business decisions in today's world. News of a leader's questionable behaviour can spread around the globe in seconds and bring down an entire organization.

Employees who trust their immediate boss have higher job satisfaction, more commitment to the company, and feel they are treated more fairly in processes and decision-making. Employees who trust their business leaders feel more committed to the company, feel the organization supports them more, and feel that leaders fairly allocate resources, treat others well, and follow procedures transparently. Trust works in different ways, depending on where you are in the organization, and C-suite leaders should focus on building different elements of trust from those needed by managers further down the organizational hierarchy.

Humans are social creatures and both historic and current findings confirm that strong, supportive communities have higher survival rates, prosper better and enjoy more content and fulfilled lives. This is also true of business communities.

Leaders today are constantly in the spotlight and are often called upon to earn authority without control. Economic and social change demands leadership by consent rather than by control. What we perceive as good leadership tends to be created by leaders, followers, and the context and purpose of the organization, and so is a collective rather than an individual responsibility.

Trust is a key ingredient of successful leadership. Trusted leaders are the guardians of the values of the organization. Trust can release the energy of people and enlarge the human and intellectual capital of employees. In a trusting environment, when we are committed to our shared purpose, we play active roles both as leaders and as followers. We talk a lot about trust these days because it tends to be a precious and scarce resource.

When we listen to the emerging needs of the workplace we step into the most relevant and useful roles and make relevant and valuable contributions, both when leading and when following. Members of organizations who are sensitive to people's reactions trust themselves and each other. They build and nurture trusting relationships and allow the future to emerge organically.

No heroic leader can resolve the complex challenges we face today. To address the important issues of our time we need a fundamental change of perspective; we need to start questioning many of our taken-for-granted assumptions about our business and social environments.

I discussed the findings of a recent The Edelman Trust Barometer report with my business partner, Mark Herbert, co-author of this book. We were intrigued, but not surprised, by its revelation that people are largely suspicious of change and innovation when they do not see the long-term benefits for all stakeholders. 54 per cent of respondents believe that business growth, money, or greed are the real impetus behind innovation, and only 27 per cent agreed that business innovates because of a desire to make the world a better place or improve people's lives. Leaders need to treat employees as adults, openly and honestly discuss the organization's challenges, and take responsibility for their decisions and actions.

Leaders also need to listen more. The trouble is that even if they want to drive key factors such as trust, most are unable to recognize – let alone change – the structural habits of attention in themselves and in their organizations. Learning to recognize our blind spots in any business culture requires a particular kind of deep personal and collective listening.

The benefits of connecting mind, heart and our senses have been well documented in both scientific and popular publications. Integrating such practices into the organizational culture increases not only the level of well-being, but also levels of trust, honesty and openness of communication.

In spite of decades of discussions and research on ethical leadership, the available information remains largely anecdotal and highly normative. Until very recently, little has been done to systematically develop the ethical leadership construct that would make it possible to test theories about its origins and outcomes within business.

This has to be questioned. Why have boards, C-suite and senior managers never questioned the moral and ethical standing of their organizations? Why is corporate governance only now beginning to address the inclusion of values that address the needs and potential of a business' largest component – people? It seems that only in times of corporate scandals and moral lapses do stakeholders and the broader public ask themselves the fundamental questions about who corporate managers are and whether they are ethical.

Being ethical is about playing fair, thinking about the welfare of others and the consequences of one's actions. However, even if one grows up with a strong sense of good or bad, the bad behaviour of others can undermine their ethical good sense. If they clear that hurdle, ethical leaders will think about the long-term consequences, drawbacks and benefits of their decisions. For the sake of being true to their own values and beliefs, they will be prepared to compete in a very different battle on the market, where the imperative is: do what is right.

Leaders are role models for their followers and model the behavioural boundaries of an organization. Appropriate and desired behaviour is promulgated through organizational culture and the socialization of newcomers. Employees learn about values from watching leaders in action. The more the leader 'walks the talk' by translating internalized values into action, the higher the level of trust and respect he generates from followers. When leaders, for the sake of acting in accordance with their values, are prepared to make personal sacrifices for followers or the company in general, employees are more willing to do the same.

Conversely, unethical behaviour by business damages not only a company's health but also its public virtues. Reputational capital is difficult to repair once it has been damaged. One driver of bad corporate behaviour by leaders who don't take ethics seriously, lies with shareholders and boards that place singular emphasis on competence and quantitative results at the expense of ethics. Technically competent leaders may get the job done and produce good quantitative results, yet still be found wanting. The fall of big organizations, such as Enron and the Lehman Brothers, has been at least partly attributed to unethical behaviour, and corporate scandals such as these have led to the call for a more ethical approach to leadership in business.

It's not just about avoiding scandal. The argument is that ethical leadership is a holistic solution that creates balance between an organization's business objectives and the well-being of employees and the wider community without threatening profitability. This theory understands the importance of trust and good relationships. In essence, modern ethical leadership theory places importance on the idea of service.

Broadly, there are three distinct approaches to leadership that each have historical and philosophical foundations emphasizing different aspects of decision-making:

Utilitarianism theory urges the leader to maximize the welfare of the subordinates. The focus is on ensuring subordinates feel good and are happy about a decision.

Libertarianism argues that a leader's primary concern is to protect the freedom of individuals. If an action or decision would constrain a subordinate's freedom, then it should be abandoned.

The third approach is based on Immanuel Kant's principle of **'doing the right thing'**. This approach says that moral and ethical actions come from understanding the rules and customs of an organization and making decisions that chime with these common, agreed values.

My final thoughts here are that a foundation in ethical practice is at the core of other leadership styles such as transformational and charismatic leadership. However, while these leadership theories demand a strong ethical outlook, the concept we call ethical leadership demands that every aspect of leadership is informed by ethical values.

Can a company be both successful and ethical? IBM's John Akers believed that market success and ethical conduct go hand in hand:

"Ethics and competitiveness are inseparable. We compete as a society. No society anywhere will compete very long or successfully with people stabbing each other in the back; with people trying to steal from each other; with everything requiring notarized confirmation because you cannot trust the other fellow; with every little squabble ending in litigation; and with government writing reams of regulatory legislation, tying business hand and foot to keep it honest."

CHAPTER FOURTEEN

From operational obsession to holistic strategy

> *"Authority—when abused through micromanagement, intimidation, or verbal or nonverbal threats—makes people shut down and productivity ceases."*
>
> John Stoker, *Overcoming Fake Talk*

As leaders return to the office after the almost universal working from home stint triggered by the pandemic, they bring experience from one of the biggest challenges of their management careers.

Managing remotely is never easy and those with a micromanagement leadership style have possibly had their eyes opened to the damage that this approach can do to the work environment. Micromanagement is a result of unhealthy communication skills.

Today's leaders have also faced, and hopefully survived, a unique challenge – staying calm in the face of a pandemic and mounting a response sufficient for the level of threat their company has faced. Any crisis is characterized by two traits: unpredictability and uncertainty. It is the mark of a true leader to not dwell on yesterday but to look ahead and plan for a more secure tomorrow. A predefined response plan is always less effective than assessing the real threat in real time and coming up with a bespoke response to minimize it.

Micromanagement is one of the most hated management flaws in business today. We have all heard the term and we know what it means even if we've never experienced it directly. But how do you know when you're becoming a micromanager? And if you suspect you are, how do you step back?

Trust more, control less.

Micromanagement is destructive leadership. It destroys trust, morale, and lines of communication. Employees disengage and creativity drops. As employees' self-esteem falls away, so does their performance. All in all, you become a large contributor to a hostile and dysfunctional work environment.

The traditional hierarchy of an organization might not be effective in containing or managing a crisis. Senior executives need to be ready to offer their teams more responsibility and liberty to make decisions that will work for their own networks of teams. They and their networks are often the very people who have the updated frontline information that will direct an effective crisis response for the organization.

For senior leaders, then, their responsibility is to ensure that they offer responsibility to the right people.

As a crisis evolves, team leaders may need to appoint more decision makers within their networks or replace those who have fallen victim to the crisis. The flexibility to appoint new temporary leaders during an emergency can build employee confidence and promote the deliberate calm that keeps operations running, irrespective of where they are and how remote they are from the hub.

Some years ago, one of my blogs tried to answer the question *Is micromanagement delusional or can it be effective?* Most out-of-the-box or disruptive ideas are badly handled by a bottom-up resource allocation process. It is top management that has to ask, 'Is there a technology under development that looks inferior or uncertain today but will undermine our business from beneath once it is properly developed?'

The notion of a top-down strategic process depends upon central control of all steps in that process. That level of control almost never exists in a large organization – quite the reverse: at the same time that corporate staff begin to plan for and roll out initiatives, operating managers are invariably already acting in ways that either undercut or enhance them.

Each leader develops techniques, procedures, and processes to accomplish their art. Seen as tools in a toolkit, they use each one when the situation dictates to generate trust, produce a vision, or motivate a subordinate to deliver their goods. In this vein, micromanagement is nothing more than another tool in your toolkit. You use it when the situation dictates. When there's a high-value, critical project underway in your area of responsibility you do not have the option of failure.

Call it self-preservation. Call it pandering. I call fulfilling the expectations of superiors, 'smart'. Micromanagement sometimes needs to be deployed to satiate superiors who themselves wield micromanagement as their normal operating mode.

But when there's space to choose a different leadership style, the following keywords are fundamental to leadership and organizational effectiveness and help us step away from micromanagement:

Trust: Trust is a key component to drive employee

engagement. Have faith in your employees and leave them room to perform. You will soon see an increase in productivity. Trust will also give you valuable feedback, while micromanagement will shut down lines of communication.

Time: Micromanagement eats time. Is it worth it? Could you do better things with your time? Should you focus on growth strategies instead of being detail-oriented?

Communication: Micromanagement shuts down communication. Your employees won't tell you what's happening for fear that they will be yet more micro-managed. Laying low will become the favoured strategy – no communication means no engagement and no growth, and you will not have the information you need to do your own job effectively.

So put trust to work, free up time and communicate.

Crafting strategy is an iterative, real-time process; commitments must be made, then either revised or stepped up as new realities emerge.

Remind yourself often of the most important question that a leader should ask: Are you placing the good of the organization first? This is the first and only valid role of a leader.

Final thought: leaders need to focus on behaviour to transform culture. Instilling new cultural characteristics requires a shift in values, mindsets and behaviours. Leaders need to model, acknowledge and recognize the behaviour that drives the desired cultural change.

To summarize, leaders are at the forefront of driving the cultural transformation within an organization. Undoubtedly, every employee plays a crucial part in the process, but ultimately it is the leaders who have the ability to set standards and lay the foundation for change and growth.

CHAPTER FIFTEEN

Organizational development: why trust and purpose is the new normal

> *"Trust is the glue of life. It's the most essential ingredient in effective communication. It's the foundational principle that holds all relationships."*
>
> Stephen R. Covey

As we said in the preface to this book, resilient leadership has been refined in the crucible of a global pandemic. With little certainty and no previous experience to draw on, CEOs have had to guide their organizations through a myriad of decisions and challenges that have had significant implications. It will take months, even years, for the full impact to become clear.

This means that clarity of thinking, communications and decision-making will continue to be at a premium. Those CEOs who can best exhibit that clarity and lead from the heart and the head will inspire their organizations to persevere through this crisis. They will position their brand to emerge in a better place, prepared for whatever else may come.

Crises like these, with deep challenges to be navigated, also lead to opportunities for learning and the building of deepened trust with all stakeholders. Handled well, they can equip organizations for a step change that creates more value not just for shareholders, but for society as a whole.

From time to time, we lose our bearings as individuals, especially when facing overwhelming challenges, as we have in these last two pandemic-stricken years. In these moments we lean into our core, our character, and personal values to find strength and focus on what really matters. Leaders facing these unprecedented times also look to their organization's core, its communal culture and values to find inspiration that will support resilience, unleash agility and help employees to not only survive but thrive.

Setting a regular cadence with a clear voice is critical. Incomplete or conflicting communications can actually slow an organization's response. So, in a time of crisis, trust is paramount. This simple formula emphasizes the key elements of trust for individuals and for organizations:

Trust = Transparency + Relationship + Experience

Trust starts with transparency: sharing what you know and admitting what you don't. Trust is also a function of relationships, some level of 'knowing' each other among you and your employees, your customers, and your ecosystem. And lastly, it depends on experience. Do you reliably do what you say? In times of growing uncertainty, trust is increasingly built by demonstrating an ability to address unanticipated situations and a steady commitment to address the needs of all stakeholders in the best way possible.

It's also important to recognize and address the emotions of all stakeholders. This is not just about charts and numbers. Narratives can be powerful ways to acknowledge the fears that naturally surface in times of crisis, while at the same time framing the opportunity that can be achieved if stakeholders come together and commit to overcoming the challenges that stand in the way.

A DataPad survey IBEM conducted asked employees about their perceptions of trust and respect in relation to their executive leadership, heads of department and their immediate line managers. The closer the manager's role was to the respondent, the more likely the employee was to answer positively. Immediate managers were trusted 'a lot' by 48 per cent of respondents, and 'a little' by 36 per cent. Just 16 per cent of immediate managers are not trusted at all.

Working with CEOs over the years, I have found that thriving cultures are those that are purpose-driven and characterized by vitality and a growth mindset. Organizations have thriving cultures when leaders are purposeful, intentional, open to personal change, and when every employee has a voice and is actively engaged in living the organization's values. Many organizations entered into this crisis with such a culture; others were struggling. But just as glass-blowing produces beautiful structures from molten sand, we have observed healthy and resilient cultures emerge from the furnace of this crisis.

How does an organization maintain or build a thriving culture in this crisis? The answer is that at their core, organizations are shadows of their leaders. Leaders who greet crisis with perspective and compassion, confront the current reality with optimism for the future, demonstrate personal resilience, and inspire that resilience among their employees are those who will make the difference.

Authentic cultures are not formed by values posted on the

wall; they are the result of leaders being purposefully committed to living those values and willing to personally change in order to model the behaviours and actions that maintain integrity. When values are real, employees and customers know the enterprise is authentic and true to its culture. Especially in a crisis, comparing actions to values is a litmus test of a company's authenticity.

Culture, we know, is the core of resilience but alone it is not enough. Our work at IBEM has shown that when organizations can accelerate performance during good times and bad, they have the capacity to mobilize, execute, and transform with agility. Agility matters more than ever. Amidst the market volatility triggered by the pandemic, a company's foresight, ability to learn, and adaptability set it apart. Companies strong in these areas have leaders who are future-focused, have a growth mindset, are able to pivot quickly in times of rapid disruption, and maintain resilience to navigate their organizations. Swift decisions to shut offices, put work from home policies in place and scale technological tools to stay connected to customers and stakeholders come only from agile leaders who have assessed the risk and pivoted quickly. They must then reassess the medium and long-term view, building on past crisis interventions and associated learnings to evolve their operation and innovate to meet changing needs. And all this while staying true to their organization's culture.

In any time, thriving organizations are true to their purpose, stick to their values and model agility. The pandemic has inevitably reduced profits all over the world and has been a searing test of every organization's culture and values. Leaders who had already laid a solid foundation for organizational culture alongside commitment to an authentic set of values had the tools they needed to hand. If they have defined and depended on an inspiring purpose, they have led through this crisis by making a difference in the lives of employees and the communities they serve. But even for those companies that hadn't yet laid the foundations for a thriving culture, this crisis also served as a crucible for change.

How, exactly? Well, quite simply, uncovering authentic organizational purpose can come from finding ways to be of service. What's needed now and at any time is for all leaders to look beyond profit and ask: 'What do I have that could help someone right now? Where can I practise abundance where there is short supply?'

Organizations will be changed when they act to make a difference in times of crisis. Connecting with employees as we enter into their home offices and living rooms, and meeting their pets and children on the screen, organically changes and strengthens those cultures. During the pandemic this happened by default and leaders can shape their cultures by design, using the lessons learned.

Amid a crisis, a company's purpose should remain steadfast. It's never negotiable. Purpose is where the head and the heart unite. It's true that many organizations have now articulated a purpose beyond profit, but purpose risks getting ignored in day-to-day decisions. In a recent survey conducted by EY, 79 per cent of business leaders believe that an organization's purpose is central to business success, yet 68 per cent said that purpose is not used as a signpost in leadership decision-making processes within their organization.

Making decisions that refer back to the organization's purpose is particularly important during a crisis, when companies are under increased pressure and stakeholders are paying close attention to every move. We know from research on purpose-driven organizations that they tend to thrive in challenging environments and times.

Purpose cultivates engaged employees. When companies are centred on an authentic purpose, employees feel that their work has meaning. Research shows that employees who feel a greater sense of connection are far more likely to ride out volatility and be there to help companies recover and grow when stability returns.

Purpose attracts loyal customers who will stick with you. Evidence-based research has shown that eight in ten consumers are more loyal to purpose-driven brands and this is what can help sustain customer relationships in a downturn and beyond.

Purpose helps companies transform in the *right* way. Companies guided by their purpose when they face hard decisions have a sharper sense of how they should evolve, and their transformation is more cohesive as a result. When purpose is put first, profits generally follow; when profits are first, the results can be more elusive.

Finally, moral and ethical leadership is the key to successful business yet it's clear from the news that the leaders of some of our most influential governments and corporations are making morally questionable decisions. These decisions put at risk the trust of society, customers and employees. Trust is the foundation of high-functioning relationships and can only be achieved by meaningful dialogue. It is clear that this is not happening. Instead we're using electronic communication where it should never be used.

Purposeful Discussions, a previous book that I authored,

discusses the relationship between communications, strategy and business development. It offers a holistic overview of the leading methods and techniques that can help guide business professionals and those in higher education through the next decade and the fourth industrial revolution.

Any period of volatility can create opportunities that businesses can leverage if they are prepared, and organizations that have been able to take a more assertive and longer-term approach to the impact of the pandemic may have also sparked innovations that will define the 'next normal'.

CHAPTER SIXTEEN

I can only imagine…

"Be courageous. I have seen many depressions in business. Always America has emerged from these stronger and more prosperous. Be as brave as your fathers before you. Have faith! Go forward!"

Thomas A. Edison, inventor and businessman

During the pandemic I decided to take a road trip. As our lockdown rules were relaxed, and after so much 'staycation', I found driving through the Surrey and Hampshire countryside on a lovely hot day very therapeutic, great for introspection, reflection and thought.

As I drove, I started to think about purpose-driven outcomes in business, the changes imposed on us all through the pandemic, the failures and successes, and one of my key topics – leadership and trust.

I have always believed that really significant lives are for extraordinary people: great saints, artists, scholars, scientists, doctors, activists, explorers, national leaders. And if ever we did discover their significance, it would in any case be incomprehensible, perhaps written in Latin or in a COBOL computer code. It wouldn't be anything that could orient or illuminate our activities. Without always acknowledging it, we are – in the background – operating with a remarkably ungenerous perspective on the meaning of life.

Perhaps I'm wrong. It is conceivable that everyone on the planet has a meaningful life in their own way; we all make choices, we all have dreams, and we all possess the ability to see out our individual outcomes and our purpose. We all trust that the choices we make drive learning, expansion and growth.

Do we lack determination, imagination, courage, and passion in today's business world?

This question brings me to the title of this chapter. It is the title of an inspiring film I saw recently based on a true story. *I Can Only Imagine* revolves around a band's lead singer who, in the film's opening scene, tells a fellow performer that he wrote the song that changed his life in only 10 minutes.

She contradicts him: "You didn't write this song in 10 minutes. It took a lifetime."

And indeed, as the story unfolds we see the lead singer's unhappy childhood with an abusive father, abandoned by an uncaring mother. "Dreams don't pay the bills," his father says. Like another of his favourite phrases – "Life hits me, I hit it back harder" – almost everything he says sounds like the title of a country song. So his son leans into an active imagination and his love of music, chasing a dream and running from broken relationships with his father and his childhood sweetheart. All he can do really well is imagine – the heart of the film.

In my first book, *Freedom After the Sharks*, I said that each of us is, to some extent or other, a reflection of the experiences of our lives. However, whether and how we succeed is determined at least in part by how we cope with those experiences and what we learn from them.

Freedom After the Sharks is the story of a man who, despite a difficult family life and professional setbacks, developed the determination, drive and skills to create a successful business and happy life. Skills and self-motivation gave this young man the drive, determination and tenacity to continue a journey through hardship to reach self-fulfilment and, ultimately, success.

We have to ask ourselves: do we give up at the first hurdle? Or do we persevere?

Every leader eventually faces difficult circumstances. In these situations, perseverance, determination and courage are key to achieving your goals. Without these traits, success becomes less likely because you don't have what it takes to persist.

There are countless examples of courageous leaders and what they all have in common is their determination to continue pushing forward despite what others believe or what circumstances throw at them. Rather than focusing on failure and becoming discouraged, courageous leaders look at challenges as opportunities to improve. Buoyed by optimism and enthusiasm, they motivate themselves to look for meaning in each challenge and turn it to their advantage. Like many other leadership skills, courage is a skill that can be learned and strengthened.

The following tips can help you to cultivate your courage and use it to increase your success.

One thing that commonly happens when you are pursuing your goals is that suddenly you'll hit a roadblock and all movement comes to a standstill. The first emotion you feel at these moments is fear, and then panic.

The Greek philosopher, Aristotle, believed courage to

be a person's most important quality: "Courage is the first of human virtues because it makes all others possible." When we are courageous, we step outside our comfort zone, leave predictability and familiarity behind, and allow ourselves to be exposed to new ideas. We can then take in new information and broaden our understanding of the world, an important tool in overcoming adversity.

Having courage enables us to stay our course when external circumstances threaten to challenge our well-being. It empowers us to confront problems head-on even if we have doubts. Through courage, we are better able to control our destiny and honour who we are and what we believe. We have a chance to avoid the even greater problems that might have been the result of not being courageous.

We develop psychological muscle when we push through fear. This gives us the strength and resilience to overcome or avoid adversity. The more we exercise this muscle, the more our self-confidence and faith will grow. We will feel empowered to confront problems head-on and courageous even in challenging times that fill us with pain and fear.

Life is about taking on challenges and overcoming hurdles and obstacles. Success lies in going beyond the boundaries and leaving no stone unturned to achieve your goals. When you believe in your purpose, you can work through obstacles, overcome disappointments and endure hardship.

John Seaman Garns, the author of *Prosperity*, once said: "Real leaders are ordinary people with extraordinary determination." Often in life, you make a journey that changes the meaning of life as you knew it. I believe every single person can be extraordinary in some way if directed correctly and if circumstances allow.

Society cannot flourish without some sense of shared purpose and belief system, and, most importantly, love. I am a firm believer in the power of curiosity and choice as the engine of fulfilment, but precisely how you arrive at your true calling is an intricate and highly individual dance of discovery.

Still, there are certain factors and certain choices on your journey of life that make it easier and more worthwhile.

Everyone has a story that tells how they have moved forward despite difficulties in family life, professional setbacks and extraordinary events like Covid-19. The journey of life is in everything we learn and we all possess the determination, passion, drive, creativity and skill build on those lessons.

As business professionals confronting the great challenges of today's business world, we have renewed responsibility for making sure our organizations do what business does best: innovate, invest and grow. We are all extraordinary and everyone has the ability to share and provide wealth creation and richness to our surroundings. The question we need to ask is how much do we want to be extraordinary?

CHAPTER SEVENTEEN

The true cost of the digital boardroom

"When your team considers only a single plan with no alternatives, alarm bells should ring. Not preparing for alternative scenarios – even the most unlikely ones – is a guarantee of being blindsided. Thinking in alternatives is not just about identifying options to an existing situation but about constantly imagining and manufacturing alternatives. By making this mindset part of your leadership team's culture, you automatically start to come up with a higher number and wider range of alternatives."

Nokia Chair Risto Siilasmaa, *On the Value of Alternative Thinking*

While lockdown was near-virtual, much was written about the impact of the pandemic on our daily lives. Confined to our homes, consumption of technology for business and leisure reached unprecedented levels. Many commentators explored how this would play out post-lockdown; reduced international travel, sustained high levels of video calls and softening demand for office space are just some examples.

For technology businesses and investors, the conversations happening in (virtual) boardrooms were most interesting. The pandemic and resulting lockdown precipitated the biggest business continuity test imaginable. And it has not gone well. The failure of large organizations to address their technical debt were thoroughly exposed.

"Keeping everyone involved when you don't have those corridor conversations and that office osmosis brings a different kind of challenge," says Andy Barratt; Former MD at Ford of Britain and Henry Ford & Son (Cork) Ltd.

Tough times often call for tough measures. So while directors were likely to be 'meeting' more often than usual to discuss and implement significant decisions around their business' response to the Covid-19 crisis, limited social contact and gatherings meant that most boards were forced to hold these important meetings virtually. Directors have had to be careful to exercise their decision-making powers in line with their company's constitution and also, from a practical perspective, make sure the virtual meetings themselves were well structured and delivered.

In general, the larger the company, the worse they have fared. Short term focus on maintaining share price combined with incentives that reward maintaining the status quo and support a 'if it ain't broke, don't fix it' mentality had left companies ill-prepared.

Meanwhile, the ongoing wave of business disruption and their resulting consequences that is being led by many technology innovations, is crashing at our shores. Boards are concerned, and rightly so, about addressing these issues before their revenue streams, brands, share values and bottom lines are negatively affected. Moreover, activist investors, regulators and other external stakeholders are starting to demand improved management of digital risk. Whether leaders fix these deficiencies themselves or are forced to, coming change is widespread and unavoidable.

NTT Security's Global Threat Intelligence Report identified a 350 per cent increase in ransomware and called out spyware as the leading malware attack tactic, indicating that hackers are in it for the long haul — waiting for the chance that they know will come.

Like them, boards also need to play the long game. This starts with understanding and governing technology-fuelled disruption. Addressing this challenge boils down to improving boardroom digital diversity. Corporate directors across industries can do this by introducing digital competencies into their boardroom and by actively developing the digital IQ of all of their board members.

Speed is everything in today's tech-driven business world. In an effort to drive up speed even more, some so-called progressive business leaders are cancelling in-person meetings in favour of the latest high-tech solutions. Yet face-to-face meetings allow for clearer communication. In addition to offering all the non-verbal information that comes from facial expressions, body language and inflection, in-person meetings also often end up being more positive and are in any case considered more credible than 'virtual' conversations.

Without non-verbal cues, there is also the risk of misinterpretation. Recent research shows, for instance, that 60 per cent of people regularly misread tone or message when communicating by email or phone.

Not only do in-person meetings tend to be more positive, they also tend to be more productive. Researchers have found that an in-person meeting generates an average 13.36 ideas; the average for a virtual meeting is 10.43. And although virtual meetings are sometimes more convenient, nearly 70 per cent of people admit to browsing social media to pass the time during audio-only conference calls.

Prioritizing speed over face time grossly underestimates the power of human interaction. If the point of business were simply to accomplish as many tasks as possible, then yes, an email would probably do. But that's not what real leadership is about. If you've ever been on the bad side of cyber miscommunication, you'll agree that faster isn't always better.

Managing a successful team and, consequently, a successful business requires personal connection and trust. Business is, in large part, about building relationships. Being a successful leader requires emotional intelligence as much as it requires drive, discipline and best practice.

Video conferencing clearly has some benefits but studies show there is simply no substitute for the face-to-face communication. Vanessa Bohns, Associate Professor of Organizational Behavior at Cornell University, has been able to quantify the difference; her research shows that face-to-face interactions are 34 times more successful than emails.

CEOs know that trust and camaraderie build great teams, create loyalty and are the basis of moving business forward. Wealth and success depend on it. That success comes from, and is built through, face-to-face interactions and experiences and cannot be replaced in the same way with virtual experiences.

"People still feel they are at a disadvantage when they are remote," says Rob Enderle, president and principal analyst at technology advisory firm Enderle Group. "Side meetings, individual breakouts and even social interaction after meetings are not addressed by current video conferencing solutions."

Technology assists us with many tasks in one way or another every single day. While technology can be an amazing and valuable tool that helps us in numerous ways, the wrong tools and apps can be incredibly frustrating. It is not unusual for people in business to see technology as both their best friend and their worst enemy. The right technology can shift the speed of board members' work from snail's pace to roadrunner. The wrong technology slows business down, exacerbates mistakes and opens up dangerous new risks. Boards become vulnerable.

The right board management governance software assures compliance, solves security issues, and enhances good governance principles. Boards become productive and efficient and are better able to keep pace with today's business practices. Essentially, the right modern governance tools set the stage for ultimate corporate success and profitability.

The wrong technology creates board meeting inefficiencies. The pace of corporate business is such that board directors can no longer wait for quarterly reports and updates. Corporate business happens in real time. Without the right technology, board directors are left out of the loop and in the dark.

Board directors need the ability to stay connected and engaged with management and the pulse of their organizations. The wrong tools and apps can hang them up.

Routine tasks simply take too long. Manual voting processes, delayed meeting RSVPs and paper processes bog down corporate secretaries. Last minute agenda changes can increase labour time and other costs greatly. Preparing agendas and board meeting minutes takes a lot of time to complete and get approved with manual processes.

Security is sorely lacking in boardrooms and in board processes. Board directors are keenly aware of the high risks of cybercrime. If it hasn't been drilled into them enough, frequent media reports of new instances of data breaches will remind them. By and large, board directors do not themselves have the IT expertise to make good first-hand decisions about how to protect the board and the company. Meanwhile, cybercrime is more sophisticated than ever. Hackers are working doggedly around the clock looking for ways to penetrate multiple layers of security.

Nearly everyone now uses email but, once again, the media tells us that personal and business email accounts and other electronic communication apps lack the necessary security to protect confidential board business. The risk of accidental disclosure to the wrong parties is ever present.

Yet boards that continue to use dated paper processes can't have the assurance that their important documents are safe. Paper documents stored in multiple locations means that it can take a long time to find the right documents and poses the risk of not being able to find them at all. Paper is more vulnerable to natural disasters such as fire and flood and to damage by vermin.

Less face-to-face interaction may save money in the short term but incurs its own costs. Many businesses have, in the past, viewed face-to-face meetings as a cost and even a luxury. It's also easier to schedule an online meeting – directors and board members can usually join in wherever they are. However, the residual trauma of the global pandemic, and particularly its enforced rationing of in-person time with one another, has helped reconfirm the value of such interactions, particularly in underpinning an organization's sense of purpose and trust. Successful leaders know that people are their most precious resource. Now they are also realizing that having those people work alongside each other in one place, at least some of the time, is a critical part of business and more important than ever before.

People cannot be fully replaced by automation; well-trained and on-the-spot employees support each other to bring case-by-case judgement to bear on every business transaction. They are another layer of security to prevent the wrong people getting access to confidential information.

Tech equipment can be complicated to use. Technical equipment can be complicated to set up and systems may be electronically incompatible with each other. Poor audio or video quality makes for unproductive meetings. Some pieces of boardroom equipment are less secure than others, setting the stage for spreading pesky viruses. If all that isn't bad enough, cybercriminals have been known to hack into boardroom cameras, placing company business at risk. An agile business needs to be sure than it is on top of its tech.

CHAPTER EIGHTEEN

Why outstanding people deserve the right company culture

> *"Any time you sincerely want to make a change, the first thing you must do is to raise your standards. Stay committed to your decisions but stay flexible in your approach."*
>
> Tony Robbins

When my book *Purposeful Discussions* was published, a colleague who is an executive director in a large FMCG (fast-moving consumer goods) company came to see me for a discussion about its premise.

In particular, he focused on an extract from the second chapter:

"When law firms, companies and others lay people off, the people who lose their jobs are generally the people who are 'good'. People who are 'outstanding' don't lose their jobs (or hardly ever). Outstanding people are the ones who bring hard work, constant improvement and greatness to whatever they do. The world needs people who are outstanding and set the highest goals possible for themselves.

Everyone can be outstanding with the right standards. If you say you cannot be outstanding, you are slapping the face of your creator. There is nothing on this earth that does not have a purpose. You are in control over what happens to you and can control it by the standards you set for yourself. Life has meaning when you give it your all.

The secret lies in the standards you set for yourself and the decisions you make. What standards are you going to choose for your life?

My colleague wanted to know how I viewed the lockdown furlough schemes that governments had put in place to make sure those whose workplaces had been shut down by the pandemic could still pay the bills. What about the inevitable redundancies that would follow – and what happens to a business forced by these exceptional circumstances to lose both outstanding and good people?

It is true that some employees are more talented than others and it's a fact of organizational life that few executives and HR managers would dispute. The more debatable point is how to treat the people who appear to have the highest potential. Opponents of special treatment argue that all employees are talented in some way and should all therefore receive equal opportunities for growth. The thinking goes that devoting a disproportionate amount of energy and resources to a select few might cause you to overlook the potential contributions of the many. But the disagreement doesn't stop there. Some executives say that a company's list of high potentials and the process for developing those on it should be a closely guarded secret. After all, why dampen motivation among the 95 per cent of employees who aren't on the list?

Recent research from the Gallup Group suggests that 87 per cent of the workforce is either not engaged (they are there physically, but not mentally or emotionally) or is totally disengaged (they actually undermine the success of an organization). This is the highest rate of disengagement ever recorded and comes at a time when 85 per cent of organizations have an employee recognition programme – which obviously isn't working. Companies spend more than $100 billion every year trying to improve employee engagement in the workplace yet employee engagement numbers remain under 35 per cent. This does matter, and it's vital that employers understand the impact employee disengagement has on overall business success.

Let's have a look at ten shocking facts on employee disengagement.

1. Fewer than three out of ten employers have an engagement strategy in place. In other words, while more than three-quarters put effort into a reactive 'employer recognition' scheme, less than a third have a proactive approach to building the engagement they want to see. A recent study by achiever.com put the proportion of companies with an established engagement strategy at just one in four. As with any other business process, engagement doesn't just happen overnight. It requires a comprehensive strategy that defines your company goals and develops techniques for fostering engagement throughout the workplace.

2. Only 30 per cent of employees feel encouraged to grow with their company. Career growth and development is significant to today's employees, especially to Millennials and Gen Z workers. In fact, opportunity for career advancement is one of the top reasons people seek new job opportunities. Yet the latest Gallup commissioned State of the American Workforce poll shows that only three in ten employees feel that their employers are concerned about their development.

3. Three-quarters of employees who move on are leaving their boss, not the company. According to a recent study, employee disengagement starts with the manager, not the company itself. The idea that quitting employees really want to leave their supervisor or manager behind should be a wake-up call to companies across the globe. It tells us why employee engagement strategies must start at the top and work their way down. Only when these strategies attempt to boost engagement at all levels within the company can employers hope to deal with employee disengagement effectively.

4. Companies with higher engagement levels have 21 per cent higher profits. Study after study shows a clear link between employee engagement and company profits. In fact, according to a study released by Forbes, companies with higher levels of employee engagement see upward of a 21 per cent increase in profits. This statistic alone should be enough to grab any business leader's attention.

5. Only 11 per cent of workers receive weekly recognition. There is a direct correlation between disengagement in the workplace and lack of recognition. Like everyone else, your employees want recognition for their hard work. Without consistent recognition, employee disengagement can skyrocket within your workplace and even your best employees will want to leave. According to our recent study at IBEM, nearly one in five employees stated their main reason for considering a new job was because they were not being recognized.

6. Employee disengagement costs companies more than $450 billion a year. According to a Harvard Business Review report, employee disengagement costs employers anywhere from $450 billion to $550 billion every year. This amounts to an incredible amount of waste within the business sector. Many employers overlook most of these expenses because they fail to see the link between higher costs and low levels of employee engagement.

7. One in five employees say that their employer never asks for feedback. Imagine trying to voice your opinion and realizing that no one is listening. That is how many employees feel, and studies show that they might be right. In our recent report on disengagement in the workplace, more than 20 per cent of respondents said that their employer was terrible at requesting feedback. In some cases, employers never asked for feedback at all.

8. Only six in 10 employees know what is expected of them. It can be nearly impossible for employees to remain engaged in the workplace if they no clear understanding of their role or the company's goals and missions. This may seem obvious – but it might be just so obvious that many employers are overlooking it. The Gallup report suggest that perhaps four in ten workers aren't really sure what their job demands of them.

9. Low employee engagement poses serious safety issues. Most employers don't relate employee engagement with workplace safety, but maybe they should. A study of the health care industry showed that providers with high engagement levels have 70 per cent fewer safety incidents than companies with lower levels of employee engagement. This improvement in workplace safety can be attributed to enhanced employee feedback processes, comprehensive employee recognition programmes, and more precise job expectations – all of which improve engagement rates.

10. Lack of inclusiveness can cause disengagement. There is good reason why 69 per cent of executives surveyed by Deloitte cited diversity and inclusion as a top priority. Deloitte's stats show that 39 per cent of employees would leave their current company for one that had a more inclusive culture, and over half (53 per cent) of Millennials would do so. A diverse workplace environment brings fresh perspective and it's important to embrace diversity and inclusion in the workplace. Understand what truly engages and motivates your employees by collecting honest feedback.

Finally, harmony in the workplace is a key factor in employee engagement. We're all familiar with the damage that can be caused by personality clashes in the workplace, but how can leaders ensure a harmonious balance between their organization and its employees?

Building a culture of engagement in which employees are seen (and see themselves) as stakeholders will promote organizational harmony, as well as creating additional financial benefits. As the Gallup study mentioned earlier found, companies with strong employee engagement saw higher productivity and this is what feeds the 20 per cent or more rise in profits. Unsurprisingly, employee retention is also significantly higher in these businesses. Engagement is, of course, a key ingredient of trust which is itself a sure foundation on which to build a culture of high performance, increasing business speed and decreasing costs.

Stephen M.R. Covey in *The Speed of Trust* captures the essence of why trust (or its lack) is at the heart of every organization's culture: "I refer to trust as the glue and the lubricant of culture. Trust is glue because it binds people together and converts routine work interactions into effective teamwork."

And, as Covey puts it, things move faster and with less expense when trust lubricates the culture. Let's test this dual concept of trust as both glue and lubricant.

Imagine for just a moment what your work culture would be like if there was absolutely no trust between you and the people in your work group:

- What if you couldn't count on others to come to work on time or stay when they were needed?
- What if you feared anything you said might be reported to the media or to your competitors?
- What would the day be like if you couldn't trust anyone to do even the simplest task without making a mistake?
- And what if the people in your group had absolutely no trust in you?

Covey's father, the educator Stephen Richards Covey, taught a very simple but powerful metaphor of trust: the emotional bank account. This metaphor of being able to make 'emotional' deposits that build trust with others carries through to the withdrawals that might diminish trust. You might want to look at the current important relationships you have within and outside your organization and consider the current state of your emotional bank account with them.

It's not all bad news. Boards are beginning to recognize and discuss the importance of building and maintaining a strong corporate culture, as recommended by the UK Financial Reporting Council's report on culture and the role of boards. But while a board itself may have a strong ethical culture, the challenge is to ensure that most people follow the lead of this 'tone at the top'. Board members have a duty to both uphold and project the company ethos, vision and behaviours.

CHAPTER NINETEEN

How trust and respect cements client relationships

"Most good relationships are built on mutual trust and respect."

Mona K. Sutphen, former White House Deputy
Chief of Staff

The world of data is constantly changing and evolving. New technologies, legislation and policies pressure companies to re-examine the way they deal with data. Developing a strategy to boost customer trust for your brand is critical to your business' long-term success. And in the wake of Covid-19, every business is now competing for customer trust.

The concept of trust is deeply hardwired in our brains. More specifically, trusting someone is associated with many positive emotions and is an amazingly persuasive force. Conversely, distrusting someone is associated with negative emotions.

How do you build trust with customers?

You earn customer trust through repeated good behaviour and providing value customers know they can't get anywhere else. In times of crisis, rather than creating new customers, you can work on maintaining your relationships with your past customers. Companies can do this by knowing their customers and finding ways to make their lives easier and better. As in any relationship, try to exploit your customer and they will run from the building.

In a post-coronavirus world, it could be a long haul back to business as usual. This is the time to think about your relationships and how to keep them healthy. Customers tend to be people of habit, and many enjoy the benefits that come from being loyal to a brand. Loyalty programmes used to only be for airlines and grocery stores but now brands across all industries offer rewards for loyalty.

A recent global technology trends report from Accenture (NYSE: ACN) suggests that leading companies that develop a people-first approach will win in today's digital economy. As technology advancements accelerate at an unprecedented rate, dramatically disrupting the workforce, companies that equip employees, partners and consumers with new skills can fully capitalize on innovations. Those that do will have unmatched capabilities to create fresh ideas, develop cutting-edge products and services, and disrupt the status quo.

Although perceived value is a strong driver to encourage shoppers to return for future products, it is not the only influence. Customer service, product range, stock availability and the shopping environment also have a key role in the shopper's decision to return.

Research by Harvard Business Review concluded that increasing customer retention by five per cent can increase company profits by between 25 and 95 per cent. Bain and Company found a direct correlation between the amount of time a customer had been with a retailer and the amount that customer spends. Their research revealed that 'apparel shoppers purchase 67 per cent more per order after shopping with a company for 30 months than they spent on their initial purchase'.

As I have said before, in the early 2000s we were all looking to deploy strategies across customer lifetime value; brand satisfaction and brand loyalty played a key part to our business survival toolbox. In today's world, customers staying loyal to companies for long periods are numbered.

How much trust consumers put in brands is decreasing all the time and they will typically now switch brands without hesitation if they get a better offer. The rule once was that 20 per cent of customers accounted for 80 per cent of turnover and this has turned into more like 40/60 and it is slowly heading towards 50/50, where loyal and disloyal customers generate much the same amount of income.

The conventional wisdom about competitive advantage is that successful companies pick a position, target a set of consumers, and configure activities to serve them better. The goal is to make customers repeat their purchases by matching the value proposition to their needs. By fending off competitors through ever-evolving uniqueness and personalization, the company can achieve sustainable competitive advantage. But the idea that purchase decisions arise from conscious choice flies in the face of much behavioural psychology.

The brain, it turns out, is not so much an analytical machine as a gap-filling machine: it takes noisy, incomplete information from the world and quickly fills in the missing pieces on the basis of past experience. Intuition, thoughts, opinions and preferences come to mind quickly and without reflection, but are strong enough to act on. This puts some fundamental, established marketing tactics in doubt – but are we as marketers powerless to stop it?

Loyalty programmes are an often overlooked aspect of customer experience, but they can be vital in building relationships and loyalty with customers when they're done well.

So exactly what is the solution?

Popular theory says there are two ways to escape the commodity market. On the one hand, a company can work more efficiently and so sell its products more cheaply. On the other, it can offer a unique added value, thereby re-establishing differentiation so that it can charge more.

If we look at the history and look at behaviour, neither of these are compelling for people who have developed brand loyalty – but how do you get customers to become loyal to your brand in the first place? Here are a few suggestions:

Build targeted messages. With social media at the centre of many people's day-to-day lives, consumers want to see that brands care about them. Consumers are constantly bombarded with ads, so yours can easily get overlooked. How do you stand out? Try targeting your ads, using campaigns that appeal to your audience's specific interests, and customizing your messages with a personal touch.

Develop a loyalty programme. Customer loyalty programmes are a huge factor in retaining loyal customers. 44 per cent of customers have two to four loyalty cards, and 25 per cent have between five to nine loyalty cards. Close to half join loyalty programmes to earn rewards, and a slightly higher proportion say it's a primary driver for their choice of a specific brand. As you can see, loyalty programmes are a huge deal with customers and it pays by getting them to come back to your brand whenever they decide to shop.

However, be aware that you're more likely to retain customers through a free rewards programme; just over half (52 per cent) aren't willing to pay a membership fee.

Adopt a mobile strategy. Brand loyalty has gone mobile. Just over three-quarters of smartphone users say that mobile offers have a positive impact on their brand loyalty, according to discount network AccessDevelopment.com. This can include surprise points and rewards or exclusive content. A further 66 per cent of consumers say they'd have a more positive opinion of a loyalty programme if it was available on their smartphone or in a mobile wallet app. Three-quarters of smartphone users are interested in having loyalty cards on their phones.

What happens if you fall behind your competitors and don't offer a mobile solution to your loyalty programme? You'll likely see a decrease in customers. Two thirds of companies that saw a decrease in customer loyalty in the past year didn't have a mobile app.

Implement feedback. Another reason a brand will lose customers is because they don't respond to the customer's needs. In today's fast-paced social landscape, customers expect brands to respond to their feedback, and quickly. Almost all customers say they're more likely to become loyal to a company that implements their feedback. By ignoring them, you're sending a message that their loyalty doesn't matter and then they're likely to move to a brand that shows them otherwise. Although ideas about brand loyalty have shifted over the last few decades, people are still brand-loyal, but what triggers that loyalty has changed. Companies need to adopt strong social and mobile strategies to retain customers who rely on the internet landscape to make buying decisions.

Let's have a look at the customer experience and why product experience management is vital.

Truly understanding customer needs may help companies improve not only the buying experience but also their bottom line. A company's relationship with its customers is about much more than improving product ratings or decreasing wait times. Understanding the customer journey is about learning what customers experience from the moment they begin considering a purchase, and then working to make the journey towards buying a product or service as simple, clear, and efficient as possible.

Customer experience has become the centrepiece of most marketing strategies today. Marketers have begun to realize that it's the biggest differentiator a brand or a retailer has in today's overcrowded market. A great customer experience starts with a compelling product experience. Customers have their pick of channels, so standing out among the crowd with relevant product information is imperative. The race to own the customer experience is on. Companies are recognizing the importance of delivering an experience that makes them stand out from their competition. Some are learning the hard way.

Finally, my personal view is that some greatly exaggerate the idea that sustainable competitive advantage has disappeared. In a world of infinite communication and innovation, many strategists seem convinced that sustainability can be delivered only by constantly making a company's value proposition the conscious consumer's rational or emotional first choice. They have forgotten, or perhaps they never understood, that the subconscious mind dominates decision-making. For fast thinkers, products and services that are easy to access and that reinforce comfortable buying habits will, over time, trump innovative but unfamiliar alternatives that may be harder to find and require the formation of new habits.

PART 3

Company growth and planning

There is no growth and no planning if there is no trust.
*This section is about the obstacles and challenges that will slow your growth.
It's about the knack the gods have for pushing your best-laid plans off track.
And it's about how bedding your leadership in a sure foundation of trust
will deliver all the manoevrability you need to navigate your way round,
over and through every difficulty. It makes hard conversations possible and
even constructive; it builds engaged and intelligently motivated teams; it
reminds us that we lead people, not assets.*

When growth is the question, trust is the answer.

CHAPTER TWENTY

Personal competency: the forgotten secret ingredient

*"'I trust you' is a better compliment than 'I love you',
because you may not always trust the person you love but
you can always love the person you trust."*

Anonymous

A few years back I came across a couple of concepts that really resonated and stuck with me. They were part of the enlightenment philosophy by which our Founding Fathers distinguished the new nation from the feudal system that they had left behind. One of these ideas that we have held onto with a passion, declaring it to be a cornerstone of the American experiment, is the concept of **personal property ownership.**

This says that through your own achievement you should have the ability to accumulate and own property regardless of your prior economic or social status. George Mason, the Founding Father who drafted the Virginia Declaration of Rights (precursor of the U.S. Declaration of Independence) set out certain inherent human rights, including 'the enjoyment of life and liberty, with the means of acquiring and possessing property'. This is the philosophical foundation of the capitalist system. We hear this principle invoked every day, especially when we feel that the government is inserting itself where it doesn't belong.

The other principle, the one that we don't hear nearly as much about, is the right of **personal competency** – the right to build your skills, express yourself and sell your products and services as you see fit. We see this expressed in words very similar to Mason's but written by Thomas Jefferson the same year. In the Declaration of Independence, Jefferson used the phrase 'life, liberty, and the pursuit of happiness'.

What's easy to forget is that these rights come with implied responsibility: what are liberty and happiness if not self-determination? How does anyone achieve self-determination without self-reliance?

Historically, people's career paths were determined by social station at birth or family occupation. In the United States, individuals had the right to pursue their dreams unfettered by those constraints. And in accepting their rights, they had to embrace the concept of personal competency; the individual oversaw life, career, and prospects.

The Industrial Revolution soon altered this model in a couple of ways. America shifted from an agrarian society to industrial, which created a new kind of feudalism; and the country ran out of territory to expand into. By the late 1800s, an increasing number of American workers saw their economic fates as predetermined, dependent on factors beyond their control and governed by policies set by the owners of mines, railroads and factories.

Prior to a series of laws that Congress passed in the first half of the twentieth century – most notably the National Labor Relations Act of 1935 – American businesses had created a new industrial serfdom in which collective bargaining was formally or informally outlawed. Although there was no formal class system, as under the old European feudal systems, members of the working class were often trapped by financial circumstance. Without employment, the workers had nothing so they had to accept the owners' terms. The economic system worked to restrict the right of personal competency.

But even after labour reforms took effect, as the number of hours in a workday and workweek were regulated, as wages and workers' standards of living rose, employers and unions together gradually built what can be seen as another, still semi-feudal model. In many ways, large corporations continued to play the role of feudal monarchs and nobility, they just did it in a kinder, gentler way. Employers created a corporate co-dependency, especially when following the models of management sage Douglas MacGregor who developed *Theory X* and the scientific management principles put forth by efficiency guru Frederick W. Taylor.

Under this outwardly seemingly benign version of feudalism, employees – as serfs – couldn't be trusted or expected to make good decisions. Management needed to dumb things down. Employees would do what they were told, and in return the nobility – or management – would take care of them. And we (management) did. We promised lifetime employment, we provided for their health care and for their retirement. I'm not going to say management did these things willingly. Organized labour played a huge role in securing workers' gains, including industrial safety, limitations on work hours and others. It does seem, though, that in a way both sides lost something in the bargain: we began to 'take care of them,' and they began to expect it.

There are those who argue today that this represents the optimal model; by putting the shareholder in first position as the primary stakeholder, wealth and prosperity will be created that will trickle down through other parts of our society.

When I entered the workforce as a manager, I was surprised at the things management didn't, or wouldn't, talk to employees about. Decisions around how business would be conducted, technology deployed, and the gains from productivity would be shared were the exclusive province of management. Even today the issue of the application of technology in the U.S. is fundamentally different from other industrial societies. Employers must negotiate the effects of technology on the workplace or working conditions, but the implementation of the technology is a voluntary or discretionary area of discussion under the National Labor Relations Act. In other industrial societies the application of the technology itself is a mandatory bargaining topic.

In the 1960s, 1970s and 1980s some interesting things came to pass. One of the first was international competition. Another significant development was that businesses found some of the costs of taking care of employees were becoming a heavy burden.

Employers began to recognize the rising cost of health care as a challenge and responded by experimenting with managed care, cost shifting, reducing benefits, and other strategies.

- Organizations that had practised no-layoff policies began to downsize their workforce, aggressively outsourcing and shipping jobs offshore.
- New defined contribution programmes like 401k plans were introduced.

- Organizations reduced or eliminated retiree health benefit programmes.

The government even participated by requiring corporate health care programmes for retirees to be primary rather than secondary to Medicare. This created even more expense for employers and contributed to the demise of retiree medical plans in many employer-sponsored plans. The decision wasn't a moral or political one, it was financial.

A shift in employee attitudes followed. The 'social contract' had been broken and employees became less trusting and less subservient.

We often hear that the latest two generations, Generation X and the Millennials, are much different as employees from previous generations: they aren't loyal to employers; they want more freedom and definition of their work and involvement; they won't allow themselves to be lured into serfdom (and for good reason).

Gen X and Millennials won't form a meaningful relationship with an employer unless they feel they are being met at least halfway. They expect the following five factors as a baseline for a desirable work environment:

- Satisfying work content
- Association with an organization that they respect and that respects them
- A mutual commitment to them and their careers
- Meaningful and timely feedback to help them improve their skills
- Equitable compensation

In addition to desiring feedback, they seek other elements in an optimal employment environment. These are the four most important:

- Maximum delegation
- Personal responsibility and 'ownership' of their projects and tasks
- Clear boundaries and a sense of the big picture
- Shared ownership (credit) for end results

Many human resources leaders and educators say that the flip side of empowerment is accountability. Isn't that what the right to personal competency means? When I think of personal competency, I think of a trust-based relationship between equals. These new generations are taking us back to the beginning.

In fairness, if society wants to fully embrace Jefferson's model, employees need to embrace the bitter with the sweet. Personal competence also implies a meritocracy; you are rewarded according to your capability and performance.

One of my colleagues has a model she refers to as *KindExcellence*™; the implication is that the two concepts in that name are fundamentally intertwined. You cannot have true kindness if you artificially lower expectations, and you can't be truly excellent if there is not compassion and consideration for the 'whole person' in your decision-making. Again, that sounds like a component of the right to personal competence.

The other important thing to remember, in concert with the principles of personal property and personal competency, is the importance of achieving balance between individual rights and societal rights. The individual doesn't have the right to pursue personal goals to the obvious and callous detriment of others. In *Federalist No. 10*, James Madison, writing under the pen-name Publius (which he shared with federalist co-authors Alexander Hamilton and John Jay) urged ratification of the U.S. Constitution because of a need for a strong central government to deal with 'great and aggregate issues' beyond the 'local and particular' matters best left to the state legislatures. Anti-federalists, writing under the pseudonym Brutus (among others) cautioned against ratification, in part because the Constitution contained no explicit guarantee of individual rights. (In one of many compromises that went into the document, Madison soon added such guarantees in the Bill of Rights.)

Tension between a need for central coordination and the ideal of personal freedom has vibrated through American political thinking ever since. That tension is also central to the health care debate. Traditional wisdom indicates that there are only two ways of delivering health care: the free market or a governmental model. I reject that premise. There is an opportunity for collaboration between individual and institutions. We can use personal competency in tandem with government and corporate responses to meet this most complex societal challenge. There is too much at stake for us to continue using old thinking to address these issues.

As economic stakeholders, Americans are giving up a significant competitive advantage as a society and as a country. The current models contain fundamental flaws that are not being addressed by any of the solutions that have been put on the table to date. They are partial and, as I said before, miss dealing with root causes and leave out key stakeholders.

CHAPTER TWENTY-ONE

A person, not a Human Resource

'I am a person – not a Human Resource!'

That statement is from a young man in a video from a UK-based movement *Engaged for Growth*, a national employee engagement initiative.

I was intrigued by the elegant simplicity of the message; I was also impressed that the UK has recognized the importance of engagement and the need for a strategy to make a difference. The young man quotes the statistic that only one in three employees in the UK is fully engaged; in the U.S. our performance is lower yet, with an average only slightly better than one in four.

So that leaves 66 per cent of employees in the UK and 75 per cent of employees in the U.S. 'mailing it in every day'.

Your reaction is 'so what?'

My reaction, as I have stated before, is that each year the Department of Labor estimates that we lose $5 trillion dollars to employee turnover. We lose another $200 billion to presenteeism. This young man in the UK advert describes how people show up but contribute less than they are capable of for a myriad of reasons, mostly to do with work-related stresses or dissatisfaction with management or other elements of their job. We spend another $100 billion on training annually, but studies estimate that the retention of that training is less than 10 per cent after 18 months.

So, you ask yourself, why? The answer lies in how we view and work with people. How many times do you hear employees referred to as human resources or human capital? As this young man clearly states, they are neither of those things; they are people.

Some of it goes back to an interesting differentiation that author and entrepreneur Seth Godin made recently between industrialists and capitalists. Industrialists use systematic solutions. They use benchmarks, standards, and best practices to seek efficiencies and squeeze more dollars out of the systems. Capitalists, on the other, hand seek to expand market opportunities. They want to grow markets and create new ones. The characteristic both share in the American economic model is that the focus is on the benefit to who they see as the primary stakeholder, the shareholder or owner.

This isn't new. I recently read Ken Follett's three-part trilogy about several families from different economic classes and countries, following them from pre-World War One through to the late 1960s. The upper-class people in the story simply don't understand how anything about the model their lives are framed by could possibly be broken. They have grown up with a sense of entitlement and sense of how things 'should be'.

A large dimension of our society still embraces this paradigm. If the wealthy and large corporations get the flexibility to do what they need to maximize shareholder return, then everyone will benefit, right? History says not necessarily. There were many who were stunned when the electorate rejected a return to this paradigm in the aftermath of war. People are still not embracing that paradigm as readily anymore. They want to be respected as individuals.

I want to be clear that I am not anti-union or anti-collective bargaining. I think an effort to prevent anyone, including public employees, from participating in the collective bargaining process is inherently flawed. I think, in fact, that individual employees should have the opportunity to choose whether to participate in that process. I think that requiring an individual to join a union before they can work for an organization or in an industry is fundamentally flawed. The union or bargaining agent, no matter what they call themselves, should be required to provide a meaningful value proposition to each prospective member, just as an employer does in their competition for talent. There should not be a mandate.

Equally, the history of the relationship between labour and management, especially in the United States, has not been an attractive one. Many employers have seen labour as a resource to be used and discarded as they saw fit.

However, to my mind collective bargaining has contributed to the concept of human resources or human capital. Under U.S. law, employers with union contracts in place are required to negotiate over wages, hours, and working conditions. They are not required to negotiate over the means of production or involve 'labour' in those discussions. It is a transaction-based, rather than relationship-based, model and in that respect, we remain unique among industrialized countries. In other countries, management is required to negotiate the introduction of new methods and technologies and not just the effects of those technologies.

I remember discussing with a Fortune 500 employer their efforts to fully implement total quality in their organization in the mid-1980s, and whether they had considered inclusion of their various collective bargaining agencies in that discussion. They were incredulous that I even asked the question; they simply saw the unions as an impediment rather than as a stakeholder.

Unions rightfully have taken much criticism for their insistence on inclusion of guarantees around economic security, pensions, and health plans that exclude personal responsibility for managing an individual's own health and they have set levels of benefits that are fiscally impossible. Societally, we have treated employees less as adults and more as immature adult children when it comes to things like retirement and the management of health.

I have expressed my concern that much of the Affordable Care Act, also known as Obamacare, focuses on the delivery of health care and the provider community instead of taking a more comprehensive view of a new role for employer and employee/ consumer. We spend more on health care than any other industrialized society for results that are tepid on average. Like the earlier examples I provided on turnover and presenteeism, these provide significant opportunities for collaboration and improvement.

I guess what I am advocating is a new model where we understand that collaboration among all the stakeholders can allow us to find solutions that benefit everybody. The studies already demonstrate that, when measured against key performance indicators, organizations that have embraced and implemented true engagement enjoy superior performance.

The systematic models – lean, black belt and so forth – have merit as tools and there is certainly room for improvement in every industry around efficiency and best practices, but foundational issues such as congruency and trust must be addressed before we see those tools implemented in a sustainable fashion.

A few years back I posed a question on LinkedIn: should we have a national engagement initiative led by a coalition of government, industry leadership and others? It did not get much interest. That was in 2008. By my calculations, if we give some validity to the estimated losses caused by employee turnover and presenteeism, we gave up $20.8 trillion in that four-year period. I will not even add in the likely benefit of managing health rather than health care delivery. It would seem to me like those dollars might have had an impact on the fiscal cliff we are facing.

As the young man said: 'I am not a human resource, I am a person'. Perhaps I overestimate the likely impact of exploring a new paradigm where we take him at his word and begin exploring a new model. Then again, perhaps not.

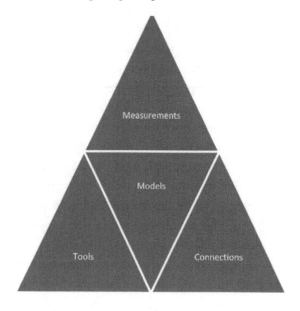

I learned painfully a number of years ago that culture eats systems. This is the stuff that makes accountants, scientists and MBAs squirm. Studies show that we tend to operate on three levels: I think, I feel, I am. Psychologist Abraham Maslow explored this in his famous hierarchy of needs. Other studies show that when our rational 'I think' conflicts with our emotional 'I feel', the emotional will prevail 85 per cent of the time. And if 'I think' conflicts with 'I am' – what Seth Godin calls our lizard brain – we are doomed! I am not dismissing the importance of systems; I am just pointing out that they do not address these emotional triggers.

Now let's consider culture.

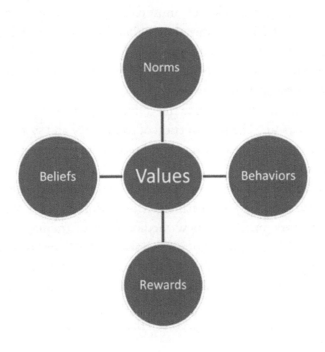

In so many cases, compliance models are based on 'do this or you will be terminated', or compensation or advancement is withheld – the win-lose model. You simply do not get sustained, excellent performance by using fear or sanctions. If you don't provide a personal upside for employees for the change you want to see – at least in the short term – it is a push and not a pull.

Much of our employment contract is based on culture but we try to address it using systemic interventions. This is why solutions like 'lean', Six Sigma, bench-marking and other change initiatives fail. You can't fix issues that have combined elements of both culture and systems using systemic interventions alone. You must address the people-y stuff.

These are not soft skills, but rather fundamental competencies that all managers and leaders must either possess or be taught to be successful. Most organizations either do a poor job of dealing with culture or they try to ignore it, focusing on technological interventions and then being puzzled and frustrated when they don't deliver sustained results.

We must learn to listen to the young man who says so clearly: 'I am a person.' The introduction of technology and systems are critical opportunities to improve, but only when accompanied by legitimacy.

A number of years ago I had an opportunity to attend a demonstration by a man named Monty Roberts who was the primary proponent of a new methodology of training horses. Although Monty is well-known in horse circles, his work is more widely known because the character played by Robert Redford in the movie *The Horse Whisperer* was based on Roberts and his methods.

Conventional wisdom has been that you break a horse in. You

teach them obedience by imposing your will on them and they learn to obey you and depend on you. Roberts' methodology was, and is, a little revolutionary. Instead, he argued, you should give a horse the opportunity to join up with you, going on to explain that horses are herd animals, and they can't survive in the wild on their own. Given the chance they have a natural proclivity to join up with other horses, or even other animals if horses are not available. As my wife is an avid horse lover, I have had a chance to see this phenomenon at first-hand.

As a human resources practitioner with years of experience, something clicked for me as I watched Monty Roberts' demonstration. Most of our employment models are, and have been, based on a compliance model. We instill obedience to a set of rules or protocols in return for security. It is a model that dates to ancient times. The powerful and rich determine appropriate behaviours and in return they afford a certain degree of security to those who comply.

Models like Frederick Taylor's *Scientific Management* reinforced that: some are born or trained to lead and others should comply.

I added Roberts' key concepts to my own thinking alongside the principles gleaned from a myriad of other models I have been exposed to, and created my own model of *Compliance to Commitment*®, which I also refer to as c2C®, or little c to big C.

My premise is that when you invite people to join up with you in support of a set of shared goals, values and benefits, you will see a much higher degree of success than if you rely on compliance. So far, experimenting with my model for over 15 years in multiple settings, I have found my premise to be accurate.

Before you get alarmed that I am espousing corporate

socialism, let me assure you I am not. My model has hierarchy, structure and expectations. Nor is it a form of corporate democracy. What it does do is say that we form a kind of covenant or contract with one another as employers and employees and we hold each other to it. It is a relationship between equals. I say equals, but not necessarily peers. Equals, to me, implies the absence of one person having some divine or societal superiority over another person. That does not mean that, as a manager, I don't have authority or greater autonomy to make decisions or set boundaries.

These days a lot of what is embedded in my model is referred to as employee engagement. There is a lot of rhetoric and discussion around engagement; its foundation is alignment. Alignment defines itself in terms of effective execution. We mesh strategy with reality, align people and talent with goals and deliver the results we commit to. The keys are that we do it willingly and proactively and we do it in furtherance of a group of shared goals and values. In that fashion it differentiates itself from a morale-building or employee satisfaction initiative. Those are outcomes of effective engagement.

Engagement is systemic. To do it successfully and sustainably involves every element of the interactions between stakeholders including customers, shareholders, employees, and communities. It is also integrated. You cannot just address one part of the equation.

Engagement is indisputably superior to other models. The results are pouring in and demonstrate that highly aligned/engaged organizations outperform their competitors in every key indicator by substantial margins. This is true across all sectors.

So, you might ask why more organizations are not endorsing and implementing an engagement strategy? There are several reasons:

- We do not yet have a common definition of engagement.
- Effective engagement is simple, but not easy. It requires both leadership and management.
- It is relationship versus technology or systemically based. You can't just install a system or a template.
- It represents a significant change from the way we have led and managed organizations for hundreds of years.
- Change and overcoming inertia is hard.

Sponsorship in most organizations has been delegated to the human resources function. There are two issues with that: one, most HR people see themselves as experts in, and responsible for, compliance not change management. Two, that kind of culture change must be driven by, and supported by, the C-suite. It is systemic and cultural, not a programme.

Engagement offers huge opportunities. The number of highly engaged employees and highly engaged organizations represents a distinct minority not only in the U.S., but internationally.

The opportunity for engagement is societal as well as industrial.

Recently I read an article about a study done by international HR consulting organization, the Hay Group. It concluded that creating an employment brand, where all stakeholder groups are represented and an integrated model is created, yields tremendous organizational success. When that model is created collaboratively by C-level leadership, marketing and human resources, it is much more effective.

I must admit my reaction was – duh! Some of us have known that for a while, although it is nice to get the validation.

"If you want to build a ship, do not drum up people together to collect wood, and don't assign them tasks and work, but rather teach them to long for the immensity of the sea."

A colleague shared Antoine de Saint-Exupery's quotation with me, and I thought it brilliantly and succinctly summarized the essence of engagement and true employment branding. As those of you familiar with my work know, I am deeply committed to a few key concepts. Among them I include building your organization on a foundation of commitment rather than compliance, and the concept of personal competency.

There are a lot of other things inherently embedded in those ideas, but they really represent the foundational pieces.

In commitment rather than compliance is the idea that when people come together proactively and willingly with a shared set of values and clarity about our purpose, the amount of energy they will bring to that effort increases exponentially. In the concept of personal competency is the idea that people are whole. They perform best when we give them both an opportunity and an expectation of being present.

My colleague Reut Schwartz-Hebron describes it in part as *KindExcellence*™. She would tell you there is not true kindness in letting someone meander through their life or career working at 70 or 80 per cent of their capacity. Neither can you achieve excellence by simply providing someone with a template and punishing them if they do it wrong.

Social gravity is the emerging concept of describing your value proposition in such a clear way and operating with such consistency that your stakeholders, including customers, employees, shareholders, suppliers and communities, are drawn to you. There is a community of interests that is clear and compelling. We have seen examples of organizations do this brilliantly, although I would argue they are few and far between.

Organizations like Apple, Starbucks, and Zippo's use social gravity. Their stakeholders self-select. They do not spend zillions of dollars on recruiting, retention or even marketing. People know what they represent and seek them out.

I read some interesting excerpts from the Steve Jobs biography. When he was questioned about being a control freak and abusive, he responded by saying: "If I was as bad as they say, do you think people would have stayed?" Individuals who chose to remain with Apple saw something greater than just Jobs and his vision. They made a cognitive choice to give up other opportunities.

Social gravity does not look the same in every organization. Since the dawn of the Industrial Revolution, we have really developed an infatuation with best practices to the point we want to use them almost like recipes. To a certain extent, the consulting sector is about promulgating templates. There are, in fact, fundamental principles followed by every organization that achieve and sustain success, but they are principles or elements that are applied uniquely to a particular setting. That is the art of leadership. I do see leadership as more of an art, whereas I see management as more of a skill.

That is not to diminish management in any way. It is a critical skill. Leadership crafts vision, but management facilitates execution; to paraphrase Seth Godin, 'long-term success in any entity is about shipping'. If no one buys your product or service or is moved by your value proposition, you had better have a plan B.

I find it interesting that we still struggle to accept this idea of social gravity. Most of our systems are based on push, not pull. We look at processes like Six Sigma, lean, TQM, and we lament that they don't guarantee long-term success.

When I see surveys concluding that most leadership failures occur because of organizational fit, interpersonal dynamics and relayed human factors, I have to say that I find the perplexity around the failure of technology to guarantee sustained success ironically amusing. The answer is right there. It isn't about processes; it is about relationships. Processes can facilitate communications and tasks, but they can't create relationships. That is a uniquely human dimension.

A technology that creates trust has yet to be developed.

When I see employers, these days requesting Facebook and other social media passwords so they can monitor employee behaviour and communications, my reaction is: "Wow, you failed the dumbass test in college, didn't you?"

To me, it is this generation's equivalent of producing tricky ways to gain access to information that the Civil Rights Act and other legislation specifically excludes us from using in employment decisions. I remember executives being very chagrined when I said: "Okay, you have obtained information that is likely non-relevant and illegal; what are you going to do with it? How about building trust instead?"

Social media provides an incredible platform that can increase your social gravity – or it can blow it sky-high. It is, however, also a tool. If you are a lousy employer, having a cool blog or website isn't going to overcome that. If you are controlling, manipulative and exploitative, monitoring the social media pages of your employees so they do not rat you out seems dumb to me. Investing in supervisory training or some therapy is a better use of your time and money.

On the other hand, if your employer says that engaging in certain behaviours, unless they are specifically protected by law, will lead to the loss of your job and you do it anyway that is, in my mind, you are failing the stupid test.

I read the story about a Marine who was discharged because he was repeatedly told that criticizing the Commander-in-Chief was a dischargeable offence and yet he did it anyway. Advocates have said his civil rights have been curtailed. Being stupid is not a protected characteristic. The orders given him to refrain from criticism were neither unlawful nor contradictory to the interests of the country or his unit. I feel similarly about people who go to foreign countries and violate their laws and customs.

For better than 100 years, our approach to the employment relationship has been to ask people to drum up wood and perform tasks; the data clearly and convincingly shows that sharing a longing for the immensity of the sea is better – way better. I know which approach I will continue to cultivate.

CHAPTER TWENTY-TWO

Measuring trust

*"Trust each other again and again. When the trust level
gets high enough, people transcend apparent limits,
discovering new and awesome abilities of which they were
previously unaware."*

David Armistead

A few years ago, I came across something called the *Edelman Trust Barometer.* For those of you not familiar with it, it was created in 2000 to measure and track the cyclical and global progress or decline of trust in four major groups: media, governmental leadership, business leadership, and non-governmental institutions or organizations. The report is published annually and provides some intriguing insights.

Although I am not primarily a data person, and as a dinosaur in my field, I find it fascinating that it is now possible to capture information scientifically about concepts such as trust and employee engagement. Areas that, when I started out in my career 40 years ago, were largely considered immeasurable. At best, they were evaluated anecdotally.

The report is ambitious in concept and execution. It collects data from tens of thousands of individuals in 28 countries and evaluates both the broader data trends and hot spots among the groups. It also confirms something that I knew anecdotally: that we continue to move in the wrong direction.

In 2017, for the first time in the history of the index, all four of the categories saw trust in them slip below 50 per cent. That year government came in last, closely followed by media, but business as the 'top' performer recorded a score of 48 per cent. Not something to be particularly enthusiastic about.

Maybe you wonder why we should care, but a quote from the book *Barbarians to Bureaucrats* captures why you might want to stop and pause: "… the decline in corporate culture precedes – and is the primary causal factor in – the decline of a business, and that decline is the result of the behaviour and spirit of its leaders."

Research from Josh Bersin, former global CEO of Deloitte, concluded that the most important things to Millennials in descending order are culture and values, career opportunities and confidence in leadership! In 2017 we began a downward trend. We saw some resurgence of trust in governmental leadership at the beginning of the response to the pandemic, but unfortunately that is no longer the case. Millennials and the groups that come after them represent not only the largest segment of the current workforce, but the future.

Some other interesting information from the 2021 edition of the index is that business is emerging as the most trusted of the four segments. In fact, in 17 of the 28 countries surveyed, trust in employers was stable or rising. Unfortunately, that is not the case in either the U.S. or the UK which both saw erosion rather than improvement. As you might suspect, the pandemic and its repercussions have exacerbated what to me was already a concerning trend.

What respondents did consistently make clear is their expectation that business, and especially its leaders, step up and take a more significant role in guiding the decision-making process and ensuring the physical and psychological safety of employees and consumers. The decline in trust in business leaders was reflected in every sector with technology, professional services and the financial sectors seeing some of the highest degradations in trust.

It is apparent, at least to me, that most organizations are clearly paying what Stephen M.R. Covey referred to as a trust tax rather than earning a trust dividend, and that technology is not the solution to the issue.

So, some things have been clearly established:

- Employee engagement is in fact real
- You will never see sustained customer engagement at higher levels than employee engagement
- The foundation of engagement is trust
- Trust is something you earn; you are not entitled to it
- Trust is a function of credibility and is made up of character, congruence, competence, and behaviour – not what you say, but how you act

A recent survey on trust by Ernst and Young involving 10,000 adults and another 3000 Gen Zers reported that fewer than 50 per cent of those surveyed trusted their employer, their immediate supervisor or their team, in descending order.

The survey sample represented four generations in the

workforce: Boomers, Gen X, Millennials and Gen Z, and the results were remarkably consistent. Although the younger generations were less trusting it wasn't a significant generational delta.

Also remarkably consistent were the environmental factors that lead to distrust:

- Perceived unfair compensation
- Unequal opportunities for pay and career advancement
- Poor leadership
- High turnover
- Lack of collaboration

Similarly, all four generations cited four characteristics they seek in a boss and organization they trust:

- Open and transparent communication
- Respect for them and other employees
- A supervisor/boss who coaches and supports their growth and advancement
- A supervisor/boss who recognizes them and their performance

High trust leadership is predicated on three fundamental characteristics that create and sustain high trust environments. Leaders who:

- listen
- demonstrate self-awareness and self-control
- demonstrate humility

Let us juxtapose that with the way most organizations identify high talent potential leaders in their organization. The selection criteria are typically:

- Professional and technical expertise
- Taking initiative and delivering results
- Honouring commitments
- Fitting into the culture

If we are honest with ourselves, we can agree that the first and last criteria are the two biggest factors. When we add the fact that 60 per cent of leadership candidates seek those opportunities to increase their earning potential and upward career trajectory, are we surprised by where we are?

In many cases we are still immersed in the precepts of Frederik Taylor's *Scientific Management* model: some were born to do, others were born to manage or lead.

Identity-based trust, Covey's highest and most critical level of trust, is nowhere to be seen in our leadership development models or development initiatives.

As an alternative I like to recommend that business leaders remember three things:

- Maslow's Hierarchy is as relevant today as it ever was. When you are in safety and survival mode you are not focusing on the big picture and how to become engaged. You are focused on basic issues like food and shelter.
- Line of sight, I tell my clients, may be the most important part of their compensation/performance management strategy. The critical function of compensation strategy

and performance management is to align efforts with outcomes. Employees need to see clearly how positive outcomes for the organization translate to positive outcomes for them and vice versa.

- Be clear with management at every level that it is their responsibility to earn and sustain trust and give them the tools to do that. They are entirely learnable and reinforceable. People rarely trust what they do not understand.

CHAPTER TWENTY-THREE

Trust and the difficult conversation

> *"A hallmark of high-performance leaders is the ability to influence others through all levels and types of communication, from simple interactions to difficult conversations and more complex conflicts, in order to achieve greater team and organizational alignment. High performing leaders are able to unite diverse team members by building common goals and even shared emotions by engaging in powerful and effective dialogue."*
>
> George Kohl

A ll leaders need to have difficult conversations at some point, whether it's telling an employee they aren't getting a raise or a promotion, disciplining poor performance or even firing someone.

Why do so many senior managers put off these conversations? And how does this then affect them, professionally and psychologically?

At one level the answer is quite simple: human beings don't like conflict and will avoid it at all costs. When our advisers are called in, we too often see managers' failure to address difficult conversations. It sometimes seems that they would rather put them off for 15 months than have a challenging 15-minute interaction and get it over with.

many line managers and leaders kick the problem off in their own minds, knowing a challenging conversation is looming and starting to play a disaster movie version of it on repeat. Every possible negative 'what if" scenario plays out in their imagination, and they start to feel under threat before any interaction has even taken place. This imaginary narrative puts increased strain on an already difficult situation. It's likely that all parties involved begin to tune into a similar mindset and this means the potential for failure whenever the conversation does eventually happen is magnified. Generally, in these circumstances, the conversation will start and end badly.

It is an understatement to say that even without these added pressures, we are already living in times of great turmoil and polarization. When unresolved conflicts permeate our lives, our workplaces, our politics, and our communities, very few systems can escape unscathed from the tension this kind of perpetual conflict generates.

At the highest levels of society, we have to watch helpless as countries use war as a strategy for settling disagreements. Our news sources are glutted with reports of violence used as a method of resolving personal and community disputes. Our schools become battle grounds as students grapple with ways to handle conflicting emotions and divergent points of view. Stories of diverted air journeys are not uncommon, sparked by a passenger who does not have the skills to deal with their own anger. Tragically, sometimes, violence breaks out in our workplaces.

Most of the time, conflict surfaces when the reaction of one or two of the people involved are so fierce that they generate strong emotions in everyone involved, even bystanders. Whether the emotions triggered within us are hot and violent or the cold chill of a disconnected relationship, most of us shy away because we don't know how to get beyond the fight-or-flight response our brains are hardwired for. Some of us can't imagine another way. We're not comfortable witnessing conflict, or experiencing it, and nor is it our first impulse to dive in and address it.

Even those of us drawn to resolving conflict may still feel that we lack the skills to handle it effectively and constructively. Generally, our associations with conflict aren't positive and we either stuff our reactions deep down or overreact and so complicate matters.

Yet conflict can, in fact, have an upside in both personal and professional settings. Properly worked with, conflict can spur innovation, creativity and a better understanding of issues and people.

Having the capacity to deal with conflict is the key to maximizing its upside. Whether the focus is delivering a difficult message, diffusing a tense situation, giving tough performance feedback, or confronting insensitive behaviour, most of us feel some reluctance when faced with the need to have challenging conversations that have the potential to escalate into conflict.

People often have misconceptions about how to handle conflict effectively, though they usually know that the basic principles are to be objective and stick to the facts. While objectivity and facts are important, our feelings surface whether we want them to or not during a challenging conversation. Feelings are a component of any situation, personal or professional. And simply sticking to the facts can block the opportunity to deal with both thoughts and emotions. Recent research shows that, in any case, people often harden their position when only dealing with the facts

To effectively deal with a difficult situation, we need to talk about our feelings and reactions in a healthy way and without blaming the other person.

If you show empathy, it doesn't mean you agree with the other person's point of view. There is a difference between empathy and agreement. It's good to let the other person know that we understand what they are saying and to acknowledge that we understand their position is true for them. This is simply respecting the person, not implying that you agree. Using phrases such as 'I understand what you're feeling, but I have a different perspective than you,' allows you to honour the person's point of view without yielding to it. While it is difficult to acknowledge the other person's point of view when you are angry or hurt, there are communication tools that can allow you to keep your cool even in the most emotionally charged situations. You can detach personally from what's being said to minimize defensiveness and optimize empathy in a way that inspires trust. So, by way of a handy guide to help you plan for a difficult conversation, here's a summary of the eight key ingredients for an honest and truthful interaction that doesn't become bogged down in recrimination.

Plan out the conversation. This is not a conversation you want to have in the spur of the moment. You want to think of what you're going to say, as well as anticipate how the other person might react. Think of the questions they might ask and have answers prepared. The more prepared you are, the easier it will be to stay even tempered and not get flustered, and therefore deliver a more solid critique.

Be direct. When having a difficult conversation, be direct and get to the point quickly. This is not the time for feedback sandwiches or compliments. Both are valid feedback techniques but will mask the point of this conversation and lessen its impact. Difficult conversations become even more difficult when the delivery is muddled. While it might seem like you're being too harsh diving right into the critique, you're actually doing the other person a favour. Most of the time, the person you're talking to knows that a critique is coming – so rather than dancing around the subject, just get to it.

Be specific. Be honest and thorough with your feedback, and fully clarify why you're having the conversation. Offer as many concrete examples as possible so the person understands you're not just pulling things out of thin air. The more clarity you can provide, the better the critique will be received.

Watch your language. The actual words you use during the conversation matter. You must outline the critique and the reason you're having the conversation, but don't stop there. You'll also want to talk about the outcome you'd like to see. If you're disciplining an employee for poor team performance, explain that to them – but also talk about what it would look like when team relations are strong. Illustrating what a positive outcome looks like gives the employee something solid to work towards and helps them understand why they're being disciplined.

Offer a solution. Nothing is worse than delivering a critique and leaving it just at that. You'll want to clearly explain the reason for the conversation, the specific critique, and then offer suggestions to improve. If you're telling an employee that they aren't getting a raise, explain why and let them know what they need to work on to make that raise a possibility. Even if the conversation is to fire an employee, you should still offer a suggestion that will help them improve in their next job.

Manage your emotions. You want to have the conversation in an even tone and keep it professional. Don't let your emotions dictate your delivery. If you get emotional, so will the other person. This is especially important when the conversation is with an employee who you care greatly for or work closely with. In this situation, take a step back and remove the relationship from the equation. It can help if you simply look at things from a fact-based standpoint and focus solely on that. When emotions start to take over, remind yourself that the more in control you are of your emotions, the better you'll be able to deliver the message.

Be empathetic. While your delivery of the message should be stoic, this doesn't mean you shouldn't empathize. Think of how the other person will feel during the conversation and allow them to process their emotions. If you see they're really struggling with what you've said, pause for a minute while they collect themselves. Clearly explain why you're having the conversation to help them fully understand where you're coming from. If they're really taking the news poorly, remind them that you're delivering this critique to make them better, and you want to see them succeed.

Allow the other person to ask questions. Questions serve a double purpose. Asking questions helps the other person process what's happened, and it allows you to clarify and solidify details of the conversation. If you aren't sure that the other person fully comprehended the conversation, ask clarifying questions to check their understanding.

One of the greatest skills managers and individuals can build is the art of listening well. This includes listening to themselves and their instincts around difficult situations as well as listening to the other person to really understand their point of view and perspective.

For managers willing to step up to the challenge, the results can be far-reaching, quicker resolution of performance issues, better work relationships, fewer grievances, reduced tension, and fewer corporate crises.

We really must build the capacity to have the challenging conversations we have often avoided. In these challenging times, the more we can master and model for others how to have challenging conversations the better our workplaces, our families, and our society will be. The choice seems clear: do we build the capacity to deal with each other in healthy ways, or do we see the world we care about deteriorate in unresolved conflicts and violence?

CHAPTER TWENTY-FOUR

Trust and team leadership

*"We all have battles to fight. And it's often in those battles
that we are most alive: it's on the frontlines of our lives
that we earn wisdom, create joy, forge friendships, discover
happiness, find love, and do purposeful work."*

Eric Greitens, former Navy SEAL and Naval
Officer

There are just a few elemental forces that hold our world together. The one that glues society together is called trust. Its presence cements relationships by allowing people to live and work together, feel safe and as if they belong. Trust in a leader allows organizations and communities to flourish, while the absence of trust can cause fragmentation, conflict and even war. That's why we need to trust our leaders, our family members, our friends and our co-workers, albeit in different ways.

Since early 2020, resilient leadership has been tested in the extreme and the challenges continue. COVID-19 has played out against a backdrop of social, political, and economic upheaval that made the terrain even harder to navigate. Challenges for leaders won't end as we try to learn to live with coronavirus. Underlying societal issues that have long been simmering below the surface are raising questions that will still be demanding answers long after the fear of pandemic has subsided. The implicit social contract between institutions and stakeholders is rightly being questioned.

Leadership is being obliged to step up in unprecedented ways. Rapid, disruptive change is today's normal. To cope, leaders need to be agile and resilient. For years, the focus has been on speed and agility but globalization, technology and social-political changes are disruptive and demand resilient, emotionally intelligent leaders able to absorb complex change, take the long-term view and help others move forward to achieve success.

Resilient organizations have sound leadership at all levels and strong cultures founded on trust, accountability, and agility. They have a foundation of meaningful core values that all members of the team believe deeply in and an exceptional sense of team unity that is uncommon in many organizations. They also have a tendency to show consistent and better-than-average profitability year after year.

Resilient leaders are well-prepared for change. Regardless of the type or magnitude of the transformation an organization is facing, one of the ultimate goals is to prepare the company for long-term strength and agility and this is a core function – possibly *the* core function – of leadership and management in the 21st century. The goal is not to simply navigate the changes in front of us, but also to create a resilient organization that is poised to meet future change; a team that is ready for the next battle – whenever that may be.

In a previous life, I spent time with Navy SEAL Teams Three and Six. Their mantra is clear: 'I serve with honour on and off the battlefield. The ability to control my emotions and my actions, regardless of circumstance, sets me apart from other men. Uncompromising integrity is my standard. My character and honour are steadfast. My word is my bond."

I am not saying all business leaders need to be trained by special forces, but the learnings for survival are transferable learnings for business. So here is the ultimate Navy SEAL guide to exceptional success and achievement, combining the key advice from some of the most storied and prolific members of this elite force. Learn their lessons, follow their lead – and you'll find you're more likely to succeed.

★★★

Develop mental toughness. Roughly 75 per cent of people who make it into the initial six-month SEAL training course, known as Basic Underwater Demolitions/SEAL Training (BUDS), don't make it through. Lars Daggars, author of *Navy SEAL Training Guide: Mental Toughness*, sets out the four pillars of mental toughness: goal-setting, mental visualization, positive self-talk, and arousal control. We'll tackle them in turn.

Set (and achieve) micro-goals. SEALs, according to Daggars, learn to focus on one thing at a time, avoiding all distractions. They do that by determining the overall objective, breaking it down into smaller pieces, and repeating as needed until they get to minute-by-minute pieces. That's the kind of planning that allowed Navy SEALs to capture and kill bin Laden – and also the same kind of strategy that can help you achieve your goals.

Visualize success (and overcoming failure). During SEALs training, there's an exercise in which students are required to accomplish a series of difficult tasks... underwater... while wearing SCUBA gear... while instructors attack them and try to destroy their equipment and keep them from breathing. Become flustered, and you fail. So, the successful ones learn to visualize ahead of time how they'll handle each calamity. As the folks at online health and well-being site *Examined Existence* wrote:

Navy psychologists discovered that those who did well and passed the exercise the first time used mental imagery to prepare them for the exercise. They imagine themselves going through the various corrective actions and they imagine doing it while being attacked.... [O]nce the exercise (and the attack) happens, the mind is ready and the [SEAL] is in full control of their physical and mental faculties.

Convince yourself you can do it. As entrepreneurs, how many times do we hear that you should fake it until you make it? That's part of how you get through SEALs training, apparently. The folks from Examined Existence sum it up like this:

Those who graduate from BUDS block all negative self-talk... and... constantly motivate themselves to keep going.... They remind themselves that should be able to pass no problem because they are more physically fit than their predecessors. They remind themselves to go on and not quit, no matter what.

Control your arousal. Arousal. Heh-heh. We're talking here about *all* kinds of sensual distractions – thinking about the lost love back home, or the things they could be doing besides training, or even the warm bed they had to leave in order to go through the day's training.

Once more, *Examined Existence*:

When our bodies feel overwhelmed or in danger, [we] release... cortisol and endorphins. These chemicals... cause our palms to sweat, our minds to race, our hearts to pound, and our bodily functions to malfunction. This is the body's natural response to stress, developed over millions of years of human evolution. But SEALS learn to control this natural response to arousal so that they are poised even under the most stressful of circumstances.

The next two tips are pretty basic, but I guess if a Navy SEAL thinks they're worth attention, they definitely work.

Be aware. If you want to be in a position to overcome danger, be aware of your surroundings. Take a photo of the slow-moving people on trains and buses each morning, obliviously checking their devices and not their surroundings. "Get your head out of your phone…. Just look up," former Navy SEAL Dom Raso once said in an interview. "It's just a very, very simple thing to do and no one does it anymore, and it's really scary."

Avoid bad stuff. This one also is obvious – so much so that former Navy SEAL Raso seems pretty upset about that others don't do it. And it goes against the uninitiated, who might believe that a Navy SEAL's first reaction is always to fight. 'Avoid, avoid, avoid,' he said. 'I want to avoid any [bad] situation before it happens.'

Given that last bit of advice, the next one makes sense

Practice humility. Success as a Navy SEAL leader means recognizing that you're not the solution to every problem. Fail to recognize that, and you're likely to flat-out fail. Jocko Willink, co-author of *Extreme Ownership: How U.S. Navy SEALs Lead and Win*, says: "The person who is not humble enough to accept responsibility when things go wrong and accept that there might be better ways to do things [has] a closed mind. They can't change, and that's what makes a person fail as a leader." Co-author Leif Babin adds: "No leader has it all figured out. You can't rely on yourself. You've got to rely on other people, so you've got to ask for help, you've got to empower the team, and you've got to accept constructive criticism."

Find your three mentors. Tim Ferriss is author of *The Four-Hour Work Week*, among other giant mega-bestsellers. He interviewed General Stanley McChrystal and McChrystal's aide, former Navy SEAL officer Chris Fussell. This key advice came from this encounter:

You should always have three people that you're paying attention to within your organization:

- Someone senior who you would like to emulate
- A peer who you think is better at the job than you are
- A subordinate who is doing your previous job better than you did

"If you just have those three individuals that you're constantly measuring yourself off of and who you're constantly learning from, you're gonna be exponentially better than you are," said Fussell.

The last items on this list come from a speech given by Admiral William McRaven, the Navy SEAL commander in charge of the raid that killed bin Laden

Do small things right. Make your bed in the morning, said McRaven. "It will give you a small sense of pride and it will encourage you to do another task and another and another. By the end of the day, that one task completed will have turned into many tasks completed. Making your bed will also reinforce the fact that little things in life matter."

Be smart about assessing others. Don't adopt others' knee-jerk assessments. McRaven talked about being in SEAL training and reflecting on a crew of physically small classmates, none of whom was more than five feet five tall. "The big men in the other boat crews would always make good natured fun of the tiny little flippers the munchkins put on their tiny little feet prior to every swim," he said. "But somehow these little guys, from every corner of the Nation and the world, always had the last laugh – swimming faster than everyone and reaching the shore long before the rest of us. SEAL training was a great equalizer."

Suck it up. This is probably the part of military training that people who've never gone through military training think of – the part they've seen in the movies where sadistic drill instructors put you through hell. McRaven talks about a punishment during SEAL training known as a 'sugar cookie.' The student had to run fully clothed into the surfzone and then, wet from head to toe, roll around on the beach until every part of your body was covered with sand…. You stayed in that uniform the rest of the day – cold, wet and sandy. The point? To learn that when you're uncomfortable and discouraged, sometimes you just have to suck it up and get through it.

Sometimes, go head first. Another McRaven story. The record for going through the SEAL obstacle course in the fastest time had stood for years. One of the trickiest parts was to manoeuvre yourself safely but quickly along a rope obstacle known as the slide for life. The record seemed unbeatable until one day a student decided to go down the slide for life – head first instead of swinging his body underneath the rope and inching his way down feet first. It was fraught with risk and failure could mean injury and being dropped from the training. It only took him half the usual time and he broke the record. In business and in any facet of life, to excel you sometimes have to accept the risks and dive in anyway.

Take on the sharks. Long before the television show, Navy SEALs learned to be afraid of sharks. There's a part of their training when they have to swim in the waters off of San Clemente, California, which they are told is a breeding ground for sharks. But if a shark begins to circle their position, they are taught to stand their ground. Do not swim away. Do not act afraid. And if the shark, hungry for a midnight snack, darts towards them, they punch him on the snout and he turns and swim away. Bandits and bullies are all around. Usually, the only way to beat them is to take them head-on.

Identify the moment that matters. One of the keys to success is consistency but, of course, we all know that some moments simply matter more than others. One of the toughest modules of SEAL is the attack on an enemy ship by swimming two miles alone, underwater, in the dark and approaching the target from below. McRaven explains: "The steel structure of the ship blocks the moonlight – it blocks the surrounding street lamps – it blocks all ambient light.. To be successful in your mission, you have to swim under the ship and find the keel – the centre line and the deepest part of the ship." The 'darkest part of the mission' is the hardest – and the most important. We all have them in our lives.

Be happy. Truth to tell, SEAL training sounds flat-out sadistic at some points. During his training, McRaven talked about his entire team being forced to stand in freezing water up to their necks, while their instructors told them they wouldn't let them out until five trainees gave up – and quit the entire course. Their reply? They started to sing. "The chattering teeth and shivering moans of the trainees were so loud it was hard to hear anything and then, one voice began to echo through the night – one voice raised in song. The song was terribly out of tune, but sung with great enthusiasm. One voice became two and two became three and before long everyone in the class was singing. We knew that if one man could rise above the misery, then others could as well." Standing in the surf and mud and freezing cold still sucked, but it sucked a little less. They gave each other hope.

Persevere – don't ring the bell. One way that SEAL training is a lot like the rest of the world is that there is an easy way to quit. You can simply give up, ring a brass bell in the middle of the compound in front of all of your peers, and walk away. All you have to do to quit is ring the bell. No more up at 5am. No more freezing cold swims. No more runs, obstacle course, PT. To end all the hardships of training, just ring the bell. "If you want to change the world, don't ever, ever ring the bell," says McRaven.

Elite Navy SEAL teams demand very high levels of performance but, in assembling their teams, team members value trust even more highly than pure performance. A trustworthy person will be selected to join a SEAL team, even if that means giving up a little bit of performance. On the other hand, individuals who are extraordinarily high performers but not trustworthy diminish the team's chances for success. Untrustworthy individual high performers are toxic to team performance, and not selected.

Re-establishing trust in all areas of life is even more critical now. Far from being a static, unchanging force, trust is dynamic and flows in multiple directions. The characteristics of being trusting and being trustworthy require us to make choices to invest in relationships that result in mutual value. Trust is a tangible exchange of value; it is actionable and human across many dimensions. So Let's examine how we can invest in, rebuild, and renew trust.

In the words of British writer George Eliot, "Those who trust us educate us." Truly building trust with our stakeholders – understanding their concerns and their priorities – involves a willingness to listen, to learn, and to hear. Building trust requires leaders to make conscious daily choices, and to act on those choices.

When we, as leaders, trust our stakeholders, we enter an exchange of **mutual trust** that engenders opportunity: we prove our own trustworthiness, and stakeholders empower our strategic choices and innovations. In essence, mutual trust creates a 'followership' that allows us to break new ground, to traverse seismic changes and emerge, thriving, on the other side of crisis.

Business leaders who are willing to be **honest about vulnerability** and acknowledge what they don't know are more likely to create trust with their stakeholders than those who mistakenly believe their greatest source of influence is in acting as though they know it all. Stakeholders are likely to regain – and even strengthen – trust in the organization when leaders admit a mistake, are apologetic, and are transparent in how they move forward.

Intent connects the leader to their humanity and the importance of acting with transparency and **authenticity**. But at the end of the day, intent is just a promise; leaders must be able to deliver it competently, reliably and capably. And they must be able to do so in the areas – whether physical, emotional, digital or financial – that matter most to their stakeholders at that given time.

Leaders who aspire to be trusted by their stakeholders **act as humans** rather than automatons. They take responsible actions that consider and, where possible, acknowledge the needs of each of those stakeholders. This requires an understanding of what is important to different stakeholders, and an ability to walk alongside them rather than an attempt to 'walk in their shoes'.

At an institutional level, value-creation discoveries, mindset shifts and collective agility bring resilient organizations and their ecosystems together into an interconnected web of resiliency and strength.

At an individual level, five of the most common traits in resilient leaders are adaptability, preparedness, collaboration, responsibility, and ethics. Adaptability and preparedness connect tomorrow's resources to potential future scenarios; collaboration connects the whole system; and responsibility and ethics connect individuals, organizations, institutions, and society.

Finally, trust-based leadership should also be understood through the lens of its influence over other leadership theories. Being trusted is a core part of other leadership, and a strong trust foundation is also needed for transformational and charismatic leadership styles. However, while a strong trust outlook is required for these leadership theories, trust leadership places the biggest emphasis on feeding trust values into every aspect of leadership.

CHAPTER TWENTY-FIVE

Purpose, trust and growth

Today's business environment is being profoundly disrupted. Volatile markets, rapid technological advances and unexpected sources of competition fuel a boiling, roiling stew of threats and opportunities, and leaders the world over are struggling to navigate this shifting landscape. Transformation is not enough. Transcendence is the new game.

So does purpose even matter? To answer that question in brief; only if it comes with clear, concise direction from top-level management and with full buy-in from mid-level management. And then, even when the company is fully aligned behind a compelling purpose, leaders must keep trust in that purpose alive by consistently modelling it from the top. You can't just adopt purpose. It has to be driven, operationally and in depth, by the CEO and the top leadership team.

The question on every leader's and executive director's mind is 'how can I be an effective leader in today's totally disruptive business world?' Companies of all sizes and in all regions of the world have reported that instilling purpose and regaining trust is the new guiding star for a world in constant flux. If the external environment is not stable, internal coherence becomes ever more vital and valuable.

To distil purpose more equally throughout an organization, many firms have considered hiring chief officers whose focus is to do exactly this. Shannon Schuyler, PwC's first-ever chief purpose officer, defines the role as connecting purpose to an individual, so they know what they need to do in their roles; and helping them see personally how they connect with the organization's values and behaviours.

When you ask employees what matters most to them, top of the list is usually the need to feel respected by superiors. Georgetown University Professor of Management Christine Porath surveyed nearly 20,000 employees worldwide and respondents ranked respect as the most important leadership behaviour. Yet each year employees report more disrespectful and uncivil behaviour from their managers.

The challenge can sometimes be finding the right balance between two different types of respect. Owed respect, the kind that all people deserve and that comes from decency and consideration for others, it obviously vital. But if it's all that's on offer, it can deflate the motivation of individuals who have gone above and beyond and feel their efforts entitle them to *earned* respect.

A survey carried out by DataPad for IBEM, for my book *Purposeful Discussions* shows that few of us trust our leaders. Few respondents to the question 'do you trust and respect your CEO?' said yes; 30 per cent responded 'not at all' and another 39 per cent responded only 'a little'. Asked the same question on the issue of trust and respect in relation to executive leaders, heads of department and immediate line managers, employees were more likely to have negative answers for those whose role was furthest away from theirs. Immediate managers were trusted 'a lot' by 48 per cent of those who responded and 'a little' by 36 per cent; 16 per cent did not trust immediate managers at all.

We all live and work in an era: a world where societies are being reshaped and.

The changes driven by increasing connectivity and public scrutiny, and by powerful global trends that disrupt business have major implications for trust. PwC in their twenty-third global CEO survey showed that CEOs are putting significant emphasis on their broader purpose and culture as they come to understand that issues such as sustainability, diversity and well-being have become business-critical.

Skills shortages are a concern everywhere and it is essential CEOs promote a company culture that complements their recruitment and retention plans, helping them attract, retain and nurture the people and the talent they need. Increasingly UK CEOs show a commitment to issues such as diversity and inclusion and the importance of well-being in the workplace. Addressing such issues not only demonstrates a commitment to workplace equality, but also reflects growing recognition that greater diversity can improve decision-making – although it is surprising that a significant proportion of businesses are yet to really focus on this issue.

To succeed, a business needs to have a clear purpose that enables people to understand why it does what it does. This purpose needs to be more than generating income. It needs to express how the business serves society. Articulating – and embracing – such a purpose has never been more important. Why? Because recent events have shaken people's trust in organizations of all types, and there have been fundamental shifts in attitudes and expectations of business. A shared recognition and understanding of why a business exists is key to bridging the trust deficit and shaping a new relationship between business and wider society.

Global accountancy firm EY describes purpose as an organization's single, underlying objective that unifies all stakeholders. Purpose should embody the company's ultimate role in the broader economic, societal, and environmental context now and decades ahead. A clear purpose goes beyond products or services and instead describes what impact or change the company can make in the largest context possible. Some examples of good purpose statements are:

- Merck: 'Our purpose is to preserve and improve human life.'
- Southwest Airlines: 'We connect people to what's important in their lives.'
- Zappos: 'Our purpose is to inspire the world by showing it's possible to simultaneously deliver happiness to customers, employees, community, vendors and shareholders in a long-term sustainable way.'

Clearly defining and articulating purpose can truly propel a company forward. Purpose helps set long-term business strategy, creates a bigger competitive advantage and differentiation in the marketplace, inspires innovation, increases brand trust and loyalty, and ultimately, helps the company stand the test of time. EY and Harvard Business Review co-authored a research project which revealed that 58 per cent of companies that are truly purpose-driven reported 10 per cent growth or more over the previous three years. The remaining 42 per cent of companies with no fully-embedded purpose reported lack of growth or even a decline in the same period.

Purpose also has the power to positively impact employees. In order for that to happen, purpose needs to be relevant, aspirational, and actively embedded in the whole company. If that's the case, a multitude of benefits materialize for employees, including trust in their organization and their own individual purpose within it.

When trust disappears, businesses can go on the defensive, stop communicating, collaborating and innovating. And that's just the start. Customer loyalty may diminish; it may get harder to attract, retain and motivate talented staff. Untrustworthy businesses may spark more regulation from the centre, adding cost and effort for everyone, and even honest businesses may lose their licence to be listened to. Together, all these factors can dampen growth, creating quantifiable impacts on share price, cost of capital and liquidity. The effects on morale, innovation and behaviour are harder to measure – but potentially even more damaging in the long-term.

Jason Lanier is one of the most celebrated pioneers of digital innovation in the world, and also one of the earliest and most prescient critics of its current trajectory. His book *Ten Arguments for Deleting Your Social Media Accounts Right Now* is as clear and definitive an account of the damage companies like Twitter, Facebook and Google do to society and to our individual psyches as you'll ever read. The book still feels relevant right now.

Lanier had been early to the idea that these platforms were addictive and even harmful – that their algorithms made people feel bad, divided them against one another, and actually changed who they were in an insidious and threatening manner. That because of this, social media was in some ways 'worse than cigarettes'. As Lanier put it: "Cigarettes don't degrade you. They kill you, but you're still you."

His most dispiriting observations are about what social media does to politics, tilting bias 'not towards the left or right, but downward'. If triggering emotions is the highest prize, and negative emotions are easier to trigger, how could social media not make you sad?

If your consumption of content is tailored by near limitless observations harvested about people like you, how could your universe not collapse into the partial depiction of reality that people like you also enjoy? How could empathy and respect for difference thrive in this environment? Where's the incentive to stamp out fake accounts, fake news, paid troll armies, dyspeptic bots?

Right now, Lanier said, most of the systems on the internet are set up to exploit us, harvesting our creative ideas and our data without compensation. The prevailing attitude in Silicon Valley is that there's no reason for you to know what your data means, how it might be used; you can't contribute, we don't know who you are, we don't want to know you, you're worthless, you're not going to get paid, it's only valuable once we aggregate it; but you know nothing, you will know nothing, you're in the dark, you're useless, you're hopeless, you're nothing. Not much trust there.

Meanwhile today's leaders today are constantly in the spotlight and are often called upon to earn authority even though they have little control. What they depend upon is leadership by consent rather than by control, and what we perceive as good leadership is often a collaborative effort between leaders, followers, and the context and purpose of whatever organization, community or society is being led – and good leadership thus becomes a collective rather than individual responsibility.

Where does trust fit into all this? Trust is a key ingredient of successful leadership. Trusted leaders are the guardians of organizational values. Trust can release energy and enlarge the human and intellectual capital of the 'collective' – in a business, the employees. In a trusting environment, when we are committed to our shared purpose, we play active roles both as leaders and as followers.

Leaders with empathetic leadership skills build trust by listening attentively to what you're telling them, putting their complete focus on the person in front of them and not getting easily distracted. They spend more time listening than talking because they want to understand the difficulties others face, all of which helps to give those around them the feeling of being heard and recognized. Empathetic executives and managers realize that the bottom line of any business is only reached through and with people. They are open to understanding the feelings and emotions of their team members.

Members of organizations who are sensitive to people's reactions trust themselves and each other. They build and nurture trusting relationships and allow the future to emerge organically.

The heroic leader cannot resolve the complex challenges we face today. To address the important issues of our time we need a fundamental change of perspective. The distant idealist cannot deliver this. Instead we need leaders who serve as role models for their followers and demonstrate the behavioural boundaries of their organization. Through culture and socialization processes, new employees learn about values from watching leaders in action. The more the leader 'walks the talk', by translating internalized values into action, the higher the level of trust and respect they generate.

So: to help bridge the trust gap, we recognize that organizations need to work with each other and with wider society to identify the practicable, actionable steps that will shape a new relationship with wider society. This is a new 'settlement' based on mutual understanding and a shared recognition of the positive role that business plays in people's lives. A clearly articulated purpose is obviously key to this.

To create such a settlement, businesses need to see themselves as part of a diverse, interconnected and interdependent ecosystem – one that involves government, regulators, individual citizens and more. Trust within and across this ecosystem is key to its long-term sustainability and survival. That's what will restore trust to the heart of the business world.

CHAPTER TWENTY-SIX

Truth, trust and work-life balance

*"Contrary to what most people believe, trust is not some
soft, illusive quality that you either have or you don't;
rather, trust is a pragmatic, tangible, actionable asset that
you can create."*

Stephen M.R Covey

The term 'work-life balance' emerged in the 1980s. We've been talking about it ever since, and particularly in recent years as millennials have increasingly dominated the younger cohorts of the workforce and employers have made tremendous efforts to appeal to them. Research from Brookings Education predicts that by 2025, the millennial generation of workers – who set great store by work-life balance – will make up 75 per cent of the workforce. Many leaders think this means it's time to redefine what that balance looks like.

In short, millennials want to be highly engaged by what they do. Smart leaders will harness that sense of mission or risk losing these employees to more purpose-driven companies.

In general terms, work-life balance is an important aspect of a healthy work environment. It helps reduce stress and prevent burnout. Chronic stress is one of the most common workplace health issues and it can have physical consequences such as hypertension, digestive troubles, chronic aches and pains and heart problems. Chronic stress can also negatively impact mental health because it's linked to a higher risk of depression, anxiety and insomnia.

The statistics clearly show a correlation between employee illness and mental health issues and too much stress over too long a period. Employees who work tons of overtime have a high risk of burnout with all the inevitable fallout that brings of fatigue, mood swings, irritability and a decrease in work performance. Harvard Business Review has suggested the psychological and physical problems of burned-out employees cost an estimated $125 billion to $190 billion a year in health care spending in the United States.

But it's important to realize that work-life balance is about more than just hours. Alongside working hours flexibility, employers should also strive to improve the overall workplace experience. Prioritizing a healthy culture and cultivating a happy workplace environment promotes work-life balance. When employees are happy in their roles, work feels more like a second home and less like the means to a pay check. Competitive compensation, comfortable office conditions, opportunities for professional growth and opportunities for social connections should all be priorities for smart leaders.

Approaches to work-life balance should evolve with cultural, generational and economic change. Flexible leaders will update or reinvent their workplace culture to try something new if employees report poor work-life balance. A constant goal is, of course, to maximize employee productivity, but ensuring employees have the time they desire away from the office and enjoy their time spent in it is a key ingredient of that. It's also the best way to retain talented employees and make them lifers, regardless of perceived generational differences.

We accept without question the need for balance in almost every other walk of life. Church bell enthusiasts know that change-ringing is the art of ringing a set of tuned tower bells in a tightly controlled manner to produce precise variations in their successive striking sequences. To achieve this, the ringer must work with the bell's momentum, applying just the right amount of effort during the pull so that the bell swings as far as required and no further. This colossal weight can be safely rung by one (experienced) ringer, but in the wrong hands the bell will lose its place in the sequence.

Pherekydes of Patrae, known in ancient Greece as the 'Giver of Rhythm', is the earliest recorded orchestra conductor. A report from 709 BC describes him leading a group of eight hundred musicians by beating a golden staff 'up and down in equal movements' so that the musicians 'began in one and the same time' and 'all might keep together'. The balanced conductor has the ability to influence the entire system of music education, which can be emulated all over the world.

Well-being, and the role that work-life balance plays in it and in the success of our businesses, has never been more important. Research from UK mental health charity Mind confirms that a culture of fear and silence around mental health costs employers dearly.

- When asked how workplace stress had affected them, more than one in five (21 per cent) employees agreed that they had called in sick to avoid work.

- 14 per cent said they had resigned and 42 per cent had considered resigning because of workplace stress.
- 30 per cent of staff disagreed with the statement 'I would feel able to talk openly with my line manager if I was feeling stressed'.
- 56 per cent of employers said they would like to do more to improve staff well-being but don't feel they have the right training or guidance.

Employers have a duty to protect the health, safety and welfare of their employees, including mental health and well-being – and doing this is good for trusted leadership and business. Certainly one of the greatest challenges for employers throughout the pandemic was finding ways to keep companies afloat while supporting the psychological well-being of their people. That challenge will not evaporate. The global health crisis has only made us all more keenly aware of the duties all organizations have to consistently assess overall levels of staff well-being and make sure frontline managers and teams remain sensitive to individual well-being. It should be a key ingredient of an organization's purpose.

Yet it has to be said that, at the leadership level, there is still a sizeable disconnect between claimed prioritization of purpose and how central purpose actually is to business decisions. Clearly leaders see the need to be purpose-driven to elevate business and are even optimistic about it, but hesitate to 'walk-the-walk' and actively embed it into the foundational decision architecture of the company.

In a time of increasingly intelligent technologies, and when an organization's ability to be trusted really matters, increasing reliance on data and AI is creating significant trust gaps, especially in the arena of health and well-being and work-life balance. Many high-profile examples of data misuse and unintended outcomes from AI usage have contributed to this mistrust because – rightly – employees see that working conditions driven in this way are unlikely to take into account the needs of humans.

Trust is an essential ingredient for well-being, life balance and mental health. Organizations must anticipate and close potential trust gaps, and work with regulators to identify practicable, actionable steps that businesses can take to shape a new relationship with wider society: a new 'settlement' based on mutual understanding and a shared recognition of the positive role that business can play in people's lives when it takes account of their well-being and what enhances their physical and mental health.

MARK'S FINAL THOUGHTS

Mutual trust: the sure foundation of a new social contract

> *Feed a person once, it elicits appreciation.*
> *Feed him twice, it creates anticipation.*
> *Feed him three times, it creates expectation.*
> *Feed him four times, it becomes an entitlement.*
> *Feed him five times, it produces dependency.*
>
> Robert D. Lupton, Charity Detox

I read this book a couple of years ago.

Although it primarily deals with the failure of our current 'charity' models in the United States and around the world, I found application for it elsewhere. Lupton talks about social entrepreneurs, people who believe that while profitable enterprise is necessary, profit that elevates the community is much more valuable than profit that only benefits a few stakeholders.

I consider myself a social entrepreneur. I remember coming across the concept a few years back when reading articles published by thinkers like Michael Porter, Nilofer Merchant, and others.

I find Lupton's writing especially poignant and current

because of the situation in my hometown. We have a significant issue with co-dependency.

For decades, the economy was based on the extraction industries, timber, and aggregates. A combination of technology, reduced demand, and environmental restrictions reduced that footprint significantly and, in many ways, the local economy has never really recovered from it. During the Clinton Administration, the Rural Schools and Community Self Determination Act was passed, providing what was intended to be temporary relief while the economy transitioned to other industries.

It was intended like spousal maintenance in a divorce, a temporary subsidy while the community transitioned. It was initially planned for six years but has been extended several times. We did not get the message and really haven't done a good job of transitioning. Although we have an excellent location and a world-class university, the biggest employers in our community are governmental agencies and not-for-profits. Not a good long-term model.

Lupton argues, and I agree, that only a strong for-profit based economy fuels stable healthy communities. He argues for what he calls holistic community development. That model measures return on investment in more than financial return to shareholders. You ask questions like:

- Is the community coming together?
- Is healthy leadership emerging?
- Is self-sufficiency increasing?

I do not blame progressive political leadership for all of where we are because corporate leaders introduced the concept of co-dependency many years back. Over two hundred years ago, some of our Founding Fathers were struggling with two related concepts as we tried to distinguish ourselves from the feudal system we had left behind; a system that split society between a ruling or ownership class and a serving class determined at birth.

The concept that broke away from this, and which we have held onto with a passion as a cornerstone of the American experiment, is that of personal property ownership – the idea that through your own achievement you should have the ability to accumulate and own property regardless of your prior economic or social status. This underpins the capitalist system, and we hear this principle invoked every day, especially when we feel that the government is inserting itself where it doesn't belong.

The other founding principle that we do not hear nearly as much about is the right of personal competency; the rights to build your skills, express yourself and sell your products and services as you see fit. This principle not only embodies a right, it implies a responsibility.

Management was not willing or able to hold up their end of the bargain for the long term. We saw parents and grandparents who had been promised lifetime employment lose their jobs. Capitalism and personal property remained but often at the expense of the American worker as we outsourced, downsized, and offshored to protect profit margins. People became a 'cost' rather than an investment. This was the birth of the concept of human capital, an expression I still despise.

That is why we continue to lose billions annually due to the costs of disengagement and the ancillary costs of unhappy, unfulfilled employees. Lupton says in *Charity Detox* that creating a co-dependent relationship with someone is the most disrespectful action you can take in a relationship. I couldn't agree more.

He goes on to make two other statements that resonate with me:

- You can't subsidize people out of poverty because you create co-dependency instead
- Education alone will not solve poverty issues

The problem with education alone is that often it creates social mobility, and the best and brightest leave their communities rather than reinvest or return.

Lupton describes a different model that he refers to as the Three Rs of Community Development:

Re-neighbouring. Under this model we create mixed-income communities. Instead of outsiders providing charity or services, you have neighbours/residents who are invested in upgrading the community because they live there!

Reconciliation. When we create economic and racial/ethnic diversity, we create neighbours who are invested in the infrastructure and success of their community.

Redistribution. Everyone in the community has something to offer and bring to the table. Interestingly, he mentions that sharing resources is much more common in less affluent neighbourhoods.

Some of this might sound like a pipe dream, but I agree with Lupton that there is no such thing as a sustainable non-profit. You may have entities that reinvest their surpluses in their mission, but organizations that can't sustain themselves are destined to fail. He recommends a model of economic missionaries, people who invest their expertise and vision and not just people who make donations. He calls it 'results-based charity'.

In our community we have a homeless issue, but many of our solutions are based on continuing a pattern of co-dependency and entitlement rather than building capacity. In fact, we have created an environment where new businesses do not care to relocate here, and existing businesses struggle because of a toxic environment.

I am not promoting purely trickle-down economics, but I am promoting more social entrepreneurialism. I would rather see us invest in vocational training and community development efforts, rather than just providing additional entitlement programmes.

Everyone is capable of contributing to their community. Those who are unwilling need to move on, not be subsidized. We are not going to build a stronger community with not-for-profits and government agencies as our economic engine. I am an advocate for personal competency, and I do not see it as someone taking care of someone else.

Anyone familiar with my writing or trainings knows I am an advocate of employee engagement or commitment over compliance. Loyalty is one of my personal pillars of an engaged relationship, but I think my definition may be different from the traditional one.

Under the old compliance model, the relationship between employer and employed had elements of what many would call loyalty. We used to see employees work for a single employer for years, perhaps even decades. The idea was that if an employee did a good job, they could expect a degree of job security that would take them through to retirement.

Maybe it is just me, but that good seemed to include a healthy dose of obedience. It was also amusing, or perhaps more ironic, that most employers who did not have unionized workforces saw employment at will as almost a sacred principle. I say 'ironic' because although employers valued this construct, they struggled with the idea that the concept of employment at will is based entirely on equal balance.

Yes, the employer can terminate any employee for any legal reason without notice or reason, but the employee also retains the right to terminate the relationship without notice or punishment.

Over my multiple decades as an HR practitioner, I spent countless hours explaining and arguing with employers that they couldn't preserve their at-will rights and then punish employees who correctly interpreted the concept and acted on it. Then, as we globalized, the concept of mutual loyalty became significantly diluted. Across the 1960s, 1970s and 1980s, you saw rightsizing, outsourcing, and a number of other approaches to cost-reduction by decreasing the size of the workforce. I personally believe this is when the concept of human capital really took root. We de-personalized people and started looking at them as an item on the balance sheet. The Millennial and Gen X generations grew up during this period. That is partly why they now view the employment relationship with such cynicism.

I grew up essentially in the Southwest, so I saw a different construct of loyalty. The Southwest is the birthplace of the cowboy. Being a cowboy wasn't just a job, it was a philosophy. It was not uncommon for cowboys to travel from ranch to ranch offering their services as required. We have an expression called 'riding for the brand'. Very loosely interpreted it meant that while I lived in your bunkhouse, ate your food, and rode your horses you had my loyalty and could reasonably expect me to give you my best efforts. It was a temporary and transitional relationship that had a degree of independence for both parties. There was mutual trust and respect on both sides.

I smile when I hear employers lament the loss of loyalty. These are often the same organizations that, during the recent recession, adjusted wages, reduced workforces and told remaining employees they should not expect, or request salary increases, but rather should be grateful to be employed.

And then the economy began improving.

Our 45th President had an interesting take on loyalty. It seems he expected, or rather demanded, personal loyalty above all else. His tumultuous relationship with Director Comey, with his chief of staff and his condemnation of his own Vice-President for certifying a lawful election result, demonstrated that he didn't define loyalty in the more widely accepted sense, but saw it rather more in the framework of absolute personal fealty. It interests me that in his own approach to loyalty, however, he is as transactional as the CEOs I have heard complain about disloyal employees.

I have personally chosen to define loyalty more in line with my cowboy roots.

First, loyalty is based on the mutual trust explained by Stephen M.R. Covey in his book, *The Speed of Trust*, at that elusive third level: identity-based trust, founded on shared values and experiences. That is the kind of trust that you hear described by members of a military unit or even an athletic team that has served or worked together. It is earned and it is reciprocated.

Second, that reciprocity is foundational and both parties see inherent value in it. We don't measure loyalty in terms of tenure, we measure it in terms of contribution. Just because someone has been with my organization for a long time it doesn't mean they are loyal. Recent studies indicated that close to 20 per cent of the U.S. workforce is actively disengaged, coming to work every day to do as little as possible and even actively disrupt or sabotage the workplace. The scary thing is these employees or no more likely to leave than employees who are neutral. They quit and stay.

Third, loyalty can be transitional. You never arrive. Like engagement, it is something you actively work at every day, and you never take it for granted.

So, I would suggest that before we require or expect loyalty, we do the work of earning our stakeholders' trust and respect and that we cultivate and nurture it. I think that Mr. Trump, like many CEOs I have known, is living in a fantasy world. You don't demand loyalty and respect; you earn them, and part of that process is that it is reciprocal and based on shared values.

We gave up the monarchy in the eighteenth century. Loyalty should be to the values and the principles embodied in the Constitution, to the office and not to the person.

I hear a lot from people that the new generations are much different from previous generations. They want more freedom and definition of their work and involvement. They don't do the old kind of loyal.

- They expect to be treated with respect and want to respect their employer
- They expect clear expectations
- They define loyalty as a mutual investment
- They focus on identity-based trust rather than trust invested in certifications or titles

In all this, I hear a trust-based relationship between equals. These 'new' generations are taking us back to the beginning. From compliance to commitment, a relationship based on respect, responsibility, information, rewards and earned loyalty, not the fealty of corporate co-dependency where obedience is rewarded with job security and retirement benefits.

In the United States, our Founding Fathers believed that alongside the principles of personal property and personal competency, we had to strike a balance between individual rights and societal rights. I do not have the right to pursue my goals to the obvious and callous detriment of others. Madison, in the famous debates between Brutus and Publius, talked about the need for a central government to deal with issues of the great and aggregate.

Let us build better models. Let us build them with respect for individual capacity and capabilities as a foundation and develop more social entrepreneurs with a focus on building stronger communities.

GEOFF'S FINAL THOUGHTS

Can we be superhuman?

*"Unless one believes in a superhuman reason which
directs evolution, one is bound to believe in a reason
inherent in humanity, a motive power transcending that
of each separate people, just as the power of the organism
transcends that of the organ. This reason increases in
proportion as the unity of mankind becomes established."*

Ellen Key, writer and early feminist thinker

I recently watched a highly recommended film, a 2011 American science fiction thriller called *Limitless* directed by Neil Burger and written by Leslie Dixon. Based on Alan Glynn's 2001 novel *The Dark Fields*, it stars Bradley Cooper, Abbie Cornish, Robert De Niro, Andrew Howard, and Anna Friel.

Limitless is as much about limits as it is about the superpower fantasy.

Its protagonist Eddie Morra is a struggling author in New York City. His girlfriend Lindy, frustrated with his lack of success, breaks up with him. Eddie encounters Vernon, the brother of his ex-wife Melissa, who gives Eddie a sample of a new nootropic – a brain-boosting superdrug – called NZT-48.

Eddie discovers the drug gives him perfect recollection of everything he has ever read along with much improved interpersonal skills. As he swallows a pill, he is being yelled at by his landlord's wife. With his new skills he calms her down, helps her with her homework, sleeps with her, and makes significant progress on his book.

The next day he takes his newly written pages to his publisher who praises them. Eddie seeks out Vernon for more NZT-48; Vernon asks him to run some errands and while Eddie is out, Vernon is murdered by someone searching for the drug. Shocked to find the body, Eddie still has the presence of mind to look for the drug himself before alerting the police and starts to take the tablets regularly. Eddie locates Vernon's supply and begins ingesting pills daily. With its effects, Eddie improves NZT-48 drives a dramatic improvement in his entire lifestyle, appearance, sex appeal and social circle improve and he finishes his book.

He has a great idea for a business, and decides to focus his talent on investing in the stock market to raise capital to fund it, and borrows $100,000 from a Russian loan shark as seed capital. Along the way, however, he is hired at a brokerage firm and resumes his relationship with Lindy. Eddie experiences what he refers to as a 'time skip', a momentary lapse in memory.

After a meeting with a finance tycoon Eddie experiences an 18 hour party-hopping time skip. The next day he sees a news bulletin about a woman who has been murdered in her hotel room – a woman he knows he slept with during his time skip.

Eddie experiments with NZT-48 so that he can learn how to control his dosage, sleep schedule and food intake to prevent side effects, he also hires a laboratory where he can reverse-engineer the drug, an attorney to keep the police from investigating the death of Vernon or the woman, and two bodyguards to protect him from the Russian loan shark who also wants NZT-48. Eddie navigates his way through a series of sinister events as everyone from the tycoon to his own attorney try to get their hands on the wonder-drug. Ultimately, Eddie makes it through – not only has he retained his wealth, but he is also running for President and has managed to wean himself off the drug and retain his abilities without side effects.

This all adds up to a great plot, brilliantly told, but it also made me think hard about how we move beyond current limits and borders. Artificial intelligence and the possibility of it rising up and taking over is a favourite topic of story telling these days – but what if humans really do become superhumans, and without AI?

Recall, for instance, the fascinating story of Jakow Trachtenberg, the man who developed a unique system of speed mathematics. He spent years in a Nazi concentration camp and to escape the horrors he endured there, he found refuge in his mind developing these methods. Some of the methods are not new and have been used for thousands of years, but he brought them together in a system of mental mathematics that makes it possible, for instance, to multiply quickly without using pen and paper. The main idea behind the Trachtenberg Speed System of Basic Mathematics is that there must be an easier way to do multiplication, division, squaring numbers and finding square roots.

So, given the extraordinary capacity of human intelligence demonstrated by people like Trachtenberg, why do we need AI, deep learning or machine learning?

The world-famous physicist Stephen Hawking had long since

warned us of the potential threat posed by artificial intelligence but more recently – and less widely reported – he had suggested that humans faced an even greater and more immediate threat. At some point in the foreseeable future, he said, the human race could divide into those with average intelligence level by today's standards, and those with super-intelligence. The latter would have bodies improved by genetic engineering and brains improved by artificial intelligence.

These 'superhumans' would be relatively few in number because genetic engineering of humans' brains and bodies will be very expensive, and only the very wealthy will be able to afford it. And they would pose a serious threat to normal humans who would become a subservient class, less healthy and less intelligent. In a few generations, the superhumans' progeny would inherit their parents' enhanced traits, making medical intervention to engineer those enhancements less necessary.

While the idea of machines becoming smarter than humans and threatening the human race is pure speculation and most experts believe it's unlikely to happen this century, if at all, the creation of superhuman beings is far less speculative. Already, humans can be improved by genetic engineering and most experts accept that greatly improving the human brain's cognitive abilities through both genetic engineering and electronic implantation will happen sooner rather than later.

When Stephen Hawking turned his thinking in this direction, he suggested that anticipated advances in genetics would enable people to acquire improved memory and intelligence, and improved disease resistance and longer lifespans. There are possibly two solutions to this: give every person the same chance to become superhuman, or ban the technology. The problem, of course is that banning the technology will just stop human evolution, and it's hard to 'un-know' a discovery.

The common take-home message is that In today's world, we are often made to feel that we have to strive for more in a commercial way, by buying things, getting a job that will pay more or moving to a bigger house in a better place. However, when we look at people who are denied these things because they're locked in, you realize that there are other, perhaps deeper ways to find happiness.

Thomas Jefferson declared that the pursuit of happiness was a universal right. But how can you define happiness? Is it material, spiritual or genetic?

So can we all be superhuman? Or is that just for a privileged few, with the rest of us destined to remain mediocre? I'd say we cannot all be superhuman – but this is not a depressing conclusion; I think we can learn from what others have accomplished and go on to make ourselves happier in our lives and do a little better. That will still improve our happiness and day-to-day existence. Even if we know we're not going to be superhuman, we can all improve and benefit from purposeful knowledge. The evidence shows the importance of attitude, and actions that have been proven to be effective will help us manage our attitude.

For the Trust Paradigm

There's no doubt that trust is imperative in any relationship and business is no different. It underpins all business relations. Trustworthy leaders drive success, put teams at ease; effective change management is based on behaviors that build trust. If trust is missing, no leadership can succeed. In an age when everything seems to be accelerating, trust is particularly difficult to build but critical. The question is how to establish it amid the ever-changing circumstances we live in today.

An important book that discusses an underestimated subject.

Patrycja Maksymowicz

Founder Open Solutions Global and London Business Academy; Startup Grind Director, Board Advisor

As a business leader myself, I believe Trust is the fruit of any relationship. This insightful book embraces the importance of people in business today and the fact that trust underpins everything we do. As many businesses have transitioned to a hybrid working culture, trust is a critical success factor. This book is a must-read for anyone looking to foster meaningful relationships.

Sophie Sayer

Sales Director and Joint Managing Executive IT Governance Publishing Ltd

As discussed in the book, Trust is critical for all businesses especially with all the "noise" of websites, social media, and SEO copywriting – every business seems to be fantastic and trustworthy – when you I know this is not true. The "eight pillars of trust" teaches leaders how to look at the process of building Trust in achievable steps. The book further inspires leaders to clearly identify the "Trust" element (or lack of) within a business – to develop it as a clear objective that is measurable and therefore improvable – the book refers to studies highlighting where "significant benefits" in every key performance indicator were achieved when organisation invest in Trust.

I love the bold notions like "Control is not Leadership" – I whole heartly believe and personally used in every role I have had since I started working – I was managing 100 people per shift at 18 using a Listen and Teaching model. "Trust Intelligence", as described in the book as well as the fifth intelligence "Wisdom Intelligence" should inspire you to shift away from 'command and control' to a 'trust and inspire' leadership model.

I not only recommend reading this book but using it as a reference as you develop and build your business on the Trust model.

Shakeeb Niazi FBCS CITP FIoEE FIET

Founder and Chair

The Society for Entrepreneurial Education and Development

The last two years have ushered in an era of tremendous change. While many businesses struggle to adapt, Geoff articulates the need for trust, one of the most fundamental aspects to any business relationship. Geoff's clarity and insights are perfect for any executive to get ahead in an ever changing world. Geoff is truly an author that "gets it" and understand what it takes to motivate people and be successful. As with all his books, I continue to learn something new that continues in both my professional and personal life. I am fortunate to have discovered an author and friend with these insights.

Scott Siegel

Global Strategy IT Leader – Capgemini

"Trust is hard to define, but we know when it's lost." – *Trust is something to be worked on and built, yet so easily lost, so prevent irreparable damage with these lessons from Geoff & Mark. An easy to consume, thought provoking catalogue of insights which will change how you do business immediately. This book is a must read for anyone in business!*

Charles Rumball, Sales Director – BCS, The Chartered Institute for IT.

"At its core, trust is an act of love. Geoff and Mark capture this truth brilliantly.

Lisa Petrilli – Sr. Director Strategic Marketing & Head of the Medline Institute

"This book is a critical reminder of the foundation of our "True North", whether that be building trust in our professional , community and personal capacities. As the world around us continues to become more complex at a faster rate, we need to leverage the trust we build to see through such complexity and in doing so continue to build a better and more sustainable future for all generations. Never before has this intangible asset of trust been so important."

Douglas Lines

Digital First Leader | Financial Services Executive

"In The Trust Paradigm Geoff and Mark discuss one of the most actual issues. Without TRUST the human essence is missing from business and without that business is not able to bring humanity forward. The Trust Paradigm is a must to read for everyone who is involved in the business world as it is high time to make a significant and holistic change. I believe that we could live in a better world if all players of the economy would follow the proposals of The Trust Paradigm."

Tamás Amer – Investment and Trade Commissioner
Economic, Investment, and Trade Section
Embassy of Hungary, London

212

"Why should you read this book? Well if you think cryptocurrencies are the first universal store of value, think again! Trust is the only truly universal currency with common, measurable value across all social, economic and political borders.

The presence of trust in a country, society or organisation leads to people choosing to settle, commit and work hard to maintain the trust paradigm as something with tangible benefit to them. Trust is the natural regulator for relationships, setting desirable standards for behaviour and engendering mutually understood boundaries. Trust creates equilibrium yet also enables all forms of progress, given that people are comfortable to take the risks required in order to advance. Each period in history characterised by peace, prosperity and progress is synonymous with a prevalence of trust. Every major brand that has enjoyed global success could not have achieved this without creating trust across cultural, political and economic borders. I would argue that the value of every intangible asset on a multinational's balance sheet is created by trust!

Conversely, the absence of trust produces dysfunctional relationships where neither party feels an obligation to regulate their behaviour since their connection has no value. The absence of trust leads to people taking action to restore this most desirable of paradigms. Consider the extreme instances of this where people will leave organisations, exit relationships, overthrow regimes or uproot themselves from their country of birth. Simply put, the absence of trust is characterised by uncertainty, conflict and ultimately chaos."

Mavric Webbstock

Senior Relationship Manager at Triodos Bank

"Trust is one of the most precious and difficult to come by resources in organizations. It requires high levels of authenticity and vulnerability as a foundation for what the authors beautifully formulate as Trust=Transperancy + Relationship + Experience. Then, in an organizational context, that intimate complexity has to be wrapped by the right decisions. This book does an amazing job of exploring the why, what, and how of this trust complexity with great clarity."

Reut Schwartz-Hebron, Certifying Partner for the Certification in Applied Neuroscience, KCI

Having had the pleasure of reading Freedom after the Sharks in which the author takes you on a real life journey of no-hidden truths about life and business. I was then keen to read Purposeful Discussions, a book that totally gripped me from start to finish. It really empathised the importance of communication, strategy, growth and planning. This book gives you the guidance as well as the tools you need to help devise effective solutions to the issues we face in business on a day-to-day basis.

I must admit that I cannot wait for the release of The Trust Paradigm, because if it is anything like the last two books I have read by this author then I know I am in for a very enjoyable read.

Stewart Elliston

Principal Head of Business Development and Associate Director at Freeths LLP

The collaborative efforts of Mark and Geoff are deep, intense, and spot on. There are so many quotes that I highlighted, but one stands out among them:

"Trust and relationships, much more than money, are the currency of business."

One particular section discusses when trust is lost, and I believe should be a class all its own for leadership. It reminded me of my last boss with whom we spent 4.5 years building a strong and effective partnership, and my trust was utterly destroyed in a single morning.

Read this book slowly enough to transform your thinking. But only if you want to significantly improve your leadership effectiveness.

Joseph Skursky – Market Leader Solutions

Resources

Buckingham, M. *The One Thing You Need to Know: About great managing, great leading, and sustained individual success*

Cormier, R. *Engaged for Growth*

Covey, Stephen M.R. *The Speed of Trust;* also *Increase trust within your team*, FranklinCovey YouTube channel, available at: https://www.youtube.com/watch?v=a0EvPEshiJs

Deming, W. Edwards *Out of the crisis: quality, productivity and competitive position; The new economics for industry, government and education*

Gladwell, M. *David and Goliath: Underdogs, Misfits and the Art of Battling Giants*

Godin, S.W. *All Marketers Are Liars: The Power of Telling Authentic Stories in a Low-Trust World* – and many other titles

Hitachi Vantara, MIT *From innovation to monetization: The economics of data-driven transformation*

Horsager, D. *The Trust Edge: How Top Leaders Gain Faster Results, Deeper Relationships, and a Stronger Bottom Line; Eight Pillars of Trust*

Isaacson, W. *Steve Jobs*

John Seaman Garns, *Prosperity Plus*

Lupton, R.D. *Charity Detox: What Charity Would Look Like if We Cared About Results*

MacGregor, D. *The Human Side of Enterprise; The Professional Manager*

217

Madison, J. *Federalist No. 10*

Malloy, O.M. *Inside the Mind of an Introvert*

Maslow, A.H. *A Theory of Human Motivation*

Matejka, K. *Why This Horse Won't Drink*

Perlow, L. *Sleeping with your Smartphone*; TED talk *'Thriving in an over connected world'*, *available at:* https://www.ted.com/talks/leslie_perlow_thriving_in_an_overconnected_world

Rumelt, R. *Good Strategy/Bad Strategy: The Difference and Why it Matters*

Schwartz-Hebron, R. *The Art and Science of Changing People Who Don't Want to Change*

Taylor, F.W. *The Principles of Scientific Management*

Warren, T.R. *White Hat Leadership: How to Maximize Personal and Employee Productivity*

Wheatley, M.J. *Leadership and the New Science*

Willink, J. and Babin, L. *Extreme Ownership: How U.S. Navy Seals Lead and Win*

This book is printed on paper from sustainable sources managed under the Forest Stewardship Council (FSC) scheme.

It has been printed in the UK to reduce transportation miles and their impact upon the environment.

For every new title that Matador publishes, we plant a tree to offset CO_2, partnering with the More Trees scheme.

For more about how Matador offsets its environmental impact, see www.troubador.co.uk/about/